# ACHIEVING YOUR DREAM CAREER

GEOFF MORGAN is currently Chairman of TMP Worldwide's Asia Pacific region. He was a founding partner of Morgan & Banks in 1985. Prior to that he was involved in the recruitment industry, initially in London and, from 1975, in Australia.

ANDREW BANKS is Global Director, eResourcing & Executive Search, TMP Worldwide. He too was a founding partner of Morgan & Banks in 1985. Prior to that he was involved in human resources management in the oil and construction industries in Australia, the UK, Norway and the USA.

They have probably interviewed, placed in jobs and counselled more people about their careers than any other duo in the business. They are passionate about the topic, having seen so many talented people struggle to find their 'dream career'.

# ACHIEVING YOUR

# DREAM

# CAREER

## GEOFF MORGAN & ANDREW BANKS

VIKING

Viking

Published by the Penguin Group
Penguin Books Australia Ltd
250 Camberwell Road, Camberwell, Victoria 3124, Australia
Penguin Books Ltd
80 Strand, London WC2R 0RL, England
Penguin Putnam Inc.
375 Hudson Street, New York, New York 10014, USA
Penguin Books, a division of Pearson Canada
10 Alcorn Avenue, Toronto, Ontario, Canada M4V 3B2
Penguin Books (NZ) Ltd
Cnr Rosedale and Airborne Roads, Albany, Auckland, New Zealand
Penguin Books (South Africa) (Pty) Ltd
24 Sturdee Avenue, Rosebank, Johannesburg 2196, South Africa
Penguin Books India (P) Ltd
11, Community Centre, Panchsheel Park, New Delhi 110 017, India

First published by Penguin Books Australia 2002

10 9 8 7 6 5 4 3 2 1

Cover design by Guy Mirabella
Text design by Louise Leffler, Penguin Design Studio
Cover image © Austral International
Typeset in 11/16 New Baskerville by Midland Typesetters, Maryborough, Victoria
Printed and bound in Australia by McPherson's Printing Group, Maryborough, Victoria

National Library of Australia
Cataloguing-in-Publication data:

Morgan, Geoff.
    Achieving your dream career.

    ISBN 0 670 91091 0.

    1. Career development.  2. Career changes.  3. Success
    I. Banks, Andrew.  II. Title.

331.702

www.penguin.com.au

*We dedicate this book to the Morgan & Banks 'family', that rich tapestry of people – clients, candidates and especially all the staff – who, over the years, helped to contribute to the success of the company, blazing a trail for the recruitment industry!*

# contents

# acknowledgements

This book has been made possible due to the support and effort of the excellent people we have been lucky enough to have around us.

# introduction

Back in the late 1990s we wrote *Getting That Job,* a book that sold tens of thousands of copies and, according to the many letters and e-mails we have received, helped thousands to find a job. Those many people who read our book and benefited from it would have noticed that nowhere in it did the words 'The End' appear.

There is a simple reason for this. Finding a job is not the end of a journey, rather it is just the beginning. In fact, we don't even like to use the word 'job'. It conjures up an image of finality, of being locked into a certain position. In reality a job is one of many dots along a line, a chapter in a long and fascinating novel, a stepping stone on the journey that is your career. It is to be hoped that each point in your career, each chapter or staging post, will be exciting and offer challenges. Indeed, some people may not feel the need to turn to the next chapter or to take the next step. They may feel fulfilled stopping where they are. *Achieving Your Dream Career* is for those who suspect they would like to push on to the next point in their career journey and are keen to write the next chapter in their professional lives. This book should help you more confidently find the right dots and stepping stones and help you to write one heck of a novel, entitled *My Dream Career*.

So what is a career? Well, if we define a job as the way you express yourself in a working environment, a career is the string that runs through and brings together a series of jobs, and a dream career would be a career in which each job is bigger, better and more fulfilling than the last one, the dots joining to form a line that truly reflects and is in synch with your abilities and aspirations.

A dream career means doing something you have dreamed about all your life – even if you didn't realise it. Your dreams may not have been as clearly defined as a picture on a TV screen. They could be abstract or no more than a vague feeling of attraction: for example, to the sea, travel, the arts, sport, the outdoors, animals, people, machines or numbers. A clue will lie in those things with which you feel comfortable. You might start your first day of paid work as a deckhand and 40 years later own a fishing boat or a fleet of fishing boats – either way feeling totally content and looking forward to the next day's work. You could begin by copying down race results in a country newspaper and eventually find yourself an editor of a national sporting magazine. You could progress from making coffee in a production house to directing a Fox Studios blockbuster or, perhaps, running a corner cafe. The journey isn't about where you end up, but how you feel when you get there, and what you experienced along the way.

Sadly, not all careers develop like a Hollywood script: the small beginning, the lucky breaks, the exciting scenes, and happy ending. What a wonderful world it would be if they did and we could all feel like jumping out of bed every morning of our working lives, punching the air with excitement and looking forward to the day's work. Imagine how productive we would become if we were all totally fulfilled by our jobs. And how much better we could become as people if, instead of merely striving to earn an extra ten dollars an hour, we made the most of our careers and simultaneously had the satisfaction of developing fully as human beings and as our true selves.

Needless to say, we don't all gulp down our breakfast every morning because we just can't wait to get to the office, and we don't all whistle while we work. That is not to say that this is an unachievable state of affairs and totally beyond our reach. To bring this about is just a matter of each person finding the direction that is right for him or her – and then being motivated to act. Everyone is capable of some kind of mastery. Having found your area of mastery you can go on to become successful and achieve your dream career. Each of us hopes to find a place where our talents can best be used and this is the key to a successful career: not stopping until you find the right path, than following it as far as you can. Like all journeys a career starts with the first step. That step has to be in the right direction, or you will find yourself walking blindly into a fog. The further you go, the deeper that fog will become and the more lost you will become. There is only one way to retrieve this situation: go back and start again. If you are not passionate about what you are doing, do something else. And if you do not know what that 'something' should be, then start looking deep within, and perhaps find someone to help you to identify it.

For many people, this is where a professional Human Resources organisation has a role to play. Its role – our role – is to raise a person's level of awareness, rather than to help them simply earn more money. We try to inspire them. If a person is mediocre at what they are doing or unhappy doing it, we pose the question: Why bother? We tell them to stop simply going through the motions day after day. We encourage them not to blame their boss or their co-workers or the colour scheme in the tearoom for their unhappiness. In short, we tell them to take charge of their life.

Time and time again we have had people in high-earning, highly respected professions (for example, doctors, lawyers and accountants) come to us after having worked for maybe as many as 20 years in their field, to tell us that all of that time they have felt that something was missing from their lives. Some of the most successful and happiest sales or marketing people we have ever placed have had medical or law degrees. What does that tell us? That just because someone has obtained the marks at school necessary to enter a certain field and even graduated in that field doesn't ensure the profession is necessarily right for them. The system might have channelled them in a certain direction, but the system doesn't take into account a little – but crucial – thing called 'suitability'.

Jobs and people are living and changing entities, so even when you are in a job that you do not actively dislike, even when you are not feeling locked in, it is a good idea to regularly reassess your position. Every two or three years you should ask yourself whether you are happy, fulfilled and getting the rewards that you need and expect from your work. Are you being challenged each day, or are you simply on cruise control operating in your comfort zone? You might consider going to a psychologist or guidance counsellor or simply buying a book on the subject of self-fulfilment. You might try a simple self-assessment questionnaire, such as the one included in this chapter (see 'For your eyes only', pp. 6–8). Do whatever it takes. We don't advise consulting the tarot cards, but if they work for you, you could try them. The fundamental thing is that you need to ask yourself: Am I happy? If the answer is yes (and remember that the criteria for employment happiness are different for each one of us), then by all means, stay put. If the answer is no, start weighing up your options. There is no law against looking around and seeing what is available for you, just as there is no longer a stigma attached to having more than one job in a lifetime. Nowadays employers are looking for more than someone who will still be on their payroll in 40 years' time. They are looking for experience – or, more precisely, experiences, life experiences.

One of the main things to remember in achieving your dream career is that it is not where you start or finish, but how far you travel on your journey. All too often people see a job as a means to an end: making money. Our experience has taught us that money is not a sign of success. It is a consequence of success. If you are happy with what you are doing, you will more likely than not do it well. If you do it well, the money and rewards will flow. It is a virtuous circle.

Take the example of an Olympic athlete. Ask them why they compete and they will not mention money. They will tell you that they perform in order to represent their country, to be the very best they can be and to strive to win that elusive gold medal. Of course, they must have talent in order to achieve their goals, but they will also need to have a deep love for what they are doing. Ambition alone won't get a swimmer to the pool before sunlight each morning to grind out the laps, nor will it be sufficient to get the runner clocking up the kilometres on a lonely road or empty training track day after day, month after month. They must want to do it; they must love doing it. Sometimes, that combination of overwhelming desire and ability will see a person reach the top of their field. The gold medal will be awarded and the money will follow – not due to the medal, but due to the passion and performance.

In sport, as in entertainment and business, there are very few overnight success stories. A pop star such as J. Lo will have worked in bars and sung in front of a handful of people for years before finally tasting fame and the millions of dollars that go with it.

A successful business might start in a one-room office or in someone's garage. Our own business has grown incrementally. In 1985 we started Morgan & Banks with one aim. Not to become rich, but to build the best business in the recruitment industry. By the time we merged with TMP Worldwide some 15 years later, we were a public company that employed 1800 people and operated 26 offices throughout Australia, New Zealand, Asia and London. With the merger, we became a fully integrated part of an organisation that is the world's leading provider of career services and solutions and employs more than 10 000 internal staff and 16 000 contract employees working from 186 offices in 32 countries. Yes, of course we made some money along the way, but this was never our primary ambition, just a by-product. We set out to do something well, to do it with passion and to enjoy the journey. We've succeeded, but the journey is not over by a long shot. There have been some tough times, sure. We have been on the brink more than once, but we were prepared to fail and we learnt to become winners. That is something you will find in most successful people. They have been brave, prepared to take risks. In some people's eyes they may have even been irresponsible or foolish, but they have found their path and followed it as far as it will take them.

And one thing that they have all discovered (as you will as you read this book and continue on your own journey): the real test comes on the day when you realise that you can afford not to jump out of bed and head off to work. But you happily do it anyway, because you realise that the life and work you love have nothing to do with making a living! The day that happens, you will have succeeded. You will have achieved your dream career.

## FOR YOUR EYES ONLY

The personal career assessment should be just that, personal. It should ask questions that only you can answer and that get right to the heart of the matter: am I satisfied with my current job and should I continue with it?

It is a good idea to put yourself through a self-assessment every two years or so, given that our circumstances, priorities and motivation are continually changing. It is also a good idea to write down both the questions and the answers. Just mentally asking yourself 'Am I happy?' is not enough. By simply sitting down and thinking of pertinent questions you will have started the assessment process. The act of writing the questions down, and then writing the answers takes the assessment to a higher plane. Very few things in life are as crucial to your long term happiness as your career. By putting yourself through a serious self-assessment and compiling your own questions and then writing out your carefully considered answers, you are giving the process the importance it deserves.

Although this is a personal undertaking and each of us will need to ask a different set of questions, a career assessment could be as simple as the one that follows.

- When I think of my current job, do I feel: Motivated? Fulfilled? Challenged? Bored? Uninspired? Trapped?
- Am I learning and growing?
- If I stay where I am, where will I be personally and professionally in: Three years? Five years? Ten years?
- What is my initial destination? (If I don't know where I'm going, I'll end up somewhere else.)
- What am I looking for in my career: Satisfaction? Learning? Excitement? Contentment? Career path? Responsibility? Stability? Wealth? Status?
- Does my current job satisfy these criteria?
- When I get ready to leave for work, do I feel: Anticipation? Excitement? Resolve? Dread? Boredom?
- Am I comfortable in my work environment? Do I feel part of

a team? Do I enjoy the company of my workmates? Do I learn from them? Do they stretch my aspirations or hold me back?

- What are the five things I like most about my job?
- What are the five things that bother me most about my job?
- Are the things I dislike about my job able to be resolved, and, if so, how?
- List five short-term and five long-term personal goals.
- Does my current job fit in with my personal goals, both short-term and long-term?
- Do I have skills that are not being fully utilised?
- Do I have skills that could be better used in another area? What are they?
- What have I done at work in the last twelve months that I am *really* proud of and that has made a difference?
- Am I really prepared to make a change?

Try to ask the questions that are important and relevant to you. Let your answers be your guide to the next step you will need to take.

## CASE STUDY
### From Actor and Wool Classer to Recruitment Specialists: Andrew Banks and Geoff Morgan

Andrew emigrated to Australia at the age of 21 after starting a degree in Behavioural Studies at London University, which he abandoned due to boredom and because he came by an Actor's Equity card and decided to pursue an acting career. His first job in Australia was playing a witch in *Macbeth* at the Sydney Opera House. He also had small parts in television soap operas and commercials.

After a year Andrew borrowed $5000 from a bank and started a restaurant. It proved highly successful and, two years later, he sold it for a considerable profit. Following this venture, Andrew got what he describes as his first real job: as personnel manager with a large French oil company. This led to a human resources position with one of the world's largest construction firms. Responsible for its European operations, he was initially based in Norway and was human resources manager for a staff of 2500, then went to Houston and finally London. It was here, as human resources manager for Europe and Africa (a division covering 6000 personnel) that Andrew's department was given the task of facilitating the evacuation of staff members following the overthrow of the Shah of Iran.

Returning to Australia in 1980, Andrew answered a newspaper advertisement calling for applicants to join the rapidly expanding executive recruitment industry. Four years later he met fellow recruiter Geoff Morgan and the pair decided to team up and start their own firm.

If it were possible to have a more roundabout entry into the industry than playing a witch at the Sydney Opera House, Geoff Morgan had it. Geoff started his working life as a wool classer. After training in Sydney, his job took him to wool-growing regions in New Zealand and throughout New South Wales and Victoria. He became involved in the Wool Classers Association, eventually taking on the role of secretary of the New South Wales branch.

After several years of learning all aspects of the wool industry, including export, it was a natural progression for Geoff to move into the new area of containerisation. He joined a large container company and was responsible for rail and road movement of containers and goods in and out of Sydney's largest clearing yards.

Whereas Andrew had come from London to Sydney to enter the recruitment industry, Geoff made the move in reverse. In London he joined a firm operating in arguably the toughest market in the world. After a year Geoff returned to Sydney, where he joined a firm specialising in the recruitment of sales and marketing personnel. Ten years later, in 1985, he and Andrew formed Morgan & Banks. Geoff says:

It would be nice to say that in 1985 we dreamed we would build our company into the success it is today. But to be honest it has evolved through us taking advantage of opportunities, seeing niches in marketplaces and acting on them. In many cases, that is what makes a dream career – being in the right place at the right time, grasping opportunities and making the most of them. Our aim in 1985 was to build the best business in the recruitment industry. Not the biggest, but the best. From that simple aim, our company grew, and with it, our careers evolved into something much richer and more rewarding than we could ever have dreamt of.

We honestly have enjoyed it every inch of the way. It hasn't always been easy, but a dream career never is. It must offer up challenges – new situations that require new solutions. A career is an ever-changing thing. Once it stops moving, it stagnates and that is when it is time to start looking for the next challenge. Happily, in our case we haven't had to go looking for the challenges. They have come looking for us.

By 1994 Morgan & Banks had become the market leader in Australia and was listed on the Sydney Stock Exchange. In 1999 the company merged with TMP Worldwide, a Nasdaq-listed company.

Andrew, as CEO, was based in New York and had global responsibility for the eResourcing Division with combined resources of US$1.2 billion, 10 000 internal staff and 16 000 contractors. He is currently Global Director for TMP Worldwide's two divisions: eResourcing and Executive Search.

Geoff, an adventurer whose passions include motor racing, heli-skiing and mountaineering, is chairman of TMP Australasia.

# chasing your dream

Dream career. It sounds so simple, doesn't it? But what does it mean? A job obviously, but more than that: a progression or series of jobs, one after the other, each ascending gently into the rarefied air of success. Like department-store escalators, you step off one, just in time to step onto the next. There's no bump, just a nice smooth ride all the way to the top.

Needless to say, it doesn't happen like that often. There are bumps, you might even get onto the wrong escalator or one that's not working and have to climb up a floor or, heaven forbid, catch another escalator that's headed down. More likely, you won't know which one to catch in the first place. Don't worry, that's normal. It is very rare to find someone who knows what they want to do with their lives from day one – and even rarer to find someone who actually does it.

But back to the question of what is a dream career? Is it a series of dream jobs? Perhaps. Then what is a dream job? It is closely related to your personal value system and the things that are important to you. It involves work that enables you to realise your value system. To discover what your value system is, simply ask yourself: What motivates me? What drives me? Chances are what you say today is different to what you would have said ten years ago and probably different to what you will say ten years from now. Usually it goes something like this. In the early days, your values are centred on learning, finding self-validation, being in a work environment and meeting new people, and, of course, having the fun of earning money for clothes, entertainment and holidays. Later, you'll probably be driven by an increasing need for professional and personal acknowledgement of your skills, further self-validation and the ongoing challenge of mastering new skills, and, of course, the financial rewards that will enable you to pay the mortgage, educate your children, buy into a good neighbourhood, and live in a safe environment where there is, ultimately, financial security.

## WHAT MAKES THE DREAM JOB?

Almost everyone has a set of specific skills and something that they can do better than anything else. It may include an ability to work with their hands or a talent to convince others to follow them. Maybe it is the knack of making the right decision at the right time. Whatever it is, the ideal is to know what your particular value system is and to know the skill set that matches that system.

If we were to put together a formula to come up with the dream job, the equation would probably go something like this: Value system plus skill set plus workplace preference equals dream job. Is there anything missing in that equation? Yes, the enjoyment factor. Just because you are good at something does not mean you actually enjoy doing it. So the dream job must maximise the things you like doing, while minimising the things you don't. It's getting a little more involved, isn't it?

Here's another element: the challenge factor. Often when people have mastered something, it no longer challenges them and they become bored and when that happens the challenge portion of the equation prevents a person from realising their dream. At other times a person's value system may change. Whereas previously it might have been enough to have the money to fly off to Tahiti at a moment's notice, it could come to pass that you now have a family and feel the need to work in a less entrepreneurial, more secure industry. Or perhaps it is your workplace preference that has changed. You need to move your job to a safer or more affordable city or to some place closer to where you live. Maybe the career path that once looked so open to advancement has been blocked by someone who isn't budging; maybe your workmate's voice has started to sound like fingernails down a blackboard. Either way, it can take only one factor to change the whole equation, throwing it out of kilter, and that is when it is time to move on. The dream job isn't a dream any more: it is too easy or insecure or inconvenient – or just plain dull. That's when it is time to step onto another escalator.

### The Dream Job Equation

Value system + skill set + workplace preference + enjoyment + challenge = DREAM JOB.

## WHAT'S IN A LABEL?

Some people would like to change the direction of their careers, yet feel trapped. More often than not, they have put a label on themselves. They think of themselves as the job they do, not the person they are.

Labels are interesting things. They can tell you a lot, or tell you nothing. Take, for instance, a 420-gram can of spaghetti at your local supermarket. Take it from the shelf and read the front of the label. Yes, it's just a can of spaghetti, all right. But when you turn the can around and look at the back, you get a clearer picture. That can contains 1680 milligrams of sodium, 630 milligrams of potassium, plus dietary fibre, sugars, carbohydrates and any number of other things. Some people never bother to read the back of the can. They don't have a need to do so. But people with allergies or on special diets depend on that list of ingredients to make their choice. So too with people's career labels.

Until the time comes to make a career change, most people rarely think about the various ingredients that go into making them who they are. They don't think of how their skills could be used in a different context. How, for example, a mother running a household could use many of the same prioritising and organisational skills to manage a business. Yet taking your particular skills and applying them differently is what can enable you to shift from one career path to another. You can use many of the same skills in a different context and start the climb on a completely different escalator that you hope will take you to your personal career goal.

## CHANGING LABELS

Think of some of the happiest, most contented people you know. Think of what they do for a living. Did they start that job the day they left school? Did they always think they would end up in the job or industry they so enjoy? Nine times out of ten, no. In some cases, they are doing jobs they didn't know existed when they left school. In many cases, those jobs actually didn't exist.

Giving the first annual Keith Murdoch Oration in Melbourne in October 2001, News Corporation chairman Rupert Murdoch, whom Bill Gates described as the most powerful man in the world, made the point that the days of 'a job for life' are long gone. Pointing out that 100 years ago a twelve-year-old boy could learn to use a tool that would equip him to make a living throughout his lifetime, Mr Murdoch said: 'At the start of the 20th century, a man could leave high school and get a job that he could keep until his retirement. Today at the start of the 21st century, it is estimated that the average working man or woman will change jobs eight times in his or her lifetime. Gradual on-the-job education is a luxury that modern turnover rates don't permit. A person must enter the work force with fundamental knowledge and core competencies that equip him or her to hold a variety of jobs – something that wasn't necessary when our parents and grandparents set out to make a living.'

The truth of Mr Murdoch's words is all around us. We just have to look past the labels. Take the film director George Miller. Did he leave school and say, 'I've got a great idea for a film. There's going to be this guy roaring around in a big car fighting baddies who are trying to steal petrol. And after I've done that, I'm thinking of a little pig who learns how to round up sheep . . .'? Of course not. George Miller is actually Dr Miller. Before *Mad Max* he thought his life was going to be spent peering down people's throats and prescribing antibiotics. He must have had a love of films, been a natural storyteller and had great vision, but getting into a position to capitalise on those raw ingredients didn't happen overnight. It took time, experience and resources to make his life's passion his life's work.

Richard Walsh was also studying medicine when he and two university friends founded the satirical magazine *Oz* in the 1960s. He headed up publishing giant Angus & Robertson before leaving to take up a senior management position in Kerry Packer's magazine empire. Rob Sitch, the man behind *Frontline, The Castle* and *The Panel,* has an MBA from Harvard Business School.

Actor Bryan Brown was a junior in an insurance company before his performance at the firm's annual Christmas show convinced him to follow his dream to the Royal Shakespeare Company, and then to star in *Breaker Morant* and *The Thorn Birds*.

Jack Welch, management guru and longtime chairman of General Electric, used to say of hiring talent that 'everyone you meet is another interview'. When his car broke down and was towed to a local garage, Jack struck up a rapport over the next two days with the mechanic. Jack was so impressed by the mechanic's determination and work ethic, as he scrambled to get parts for the repair work, that he hired him. The former mechanic was still working his way up through the organisation 35 years later. Similarly, three lawyers that Welch hired were all eventually seen to have strengths beyond GE's legal department. Welch recognised their abilities and encouraged them to concentrate on the business side of the corporation. One became head of GE's aviation finance operation; and another took charge of the company's business development; and the third became president of GE Japan. Incidentally, Jack Welch, who is seen to be the quintessential CEO, has a Ph.D. in chemical engineering. Did he always want to be a success? Of course. Did he always have a talent for management and natural leadership? Undoubtedly. It is just that he took an indirect route to get to where he wanted to go.

Author Peter Carey is another case in point. He didn't start out as a writer and the road he took getting to the top of the literary world was a circuitous one. The man who in October 2001 won his second Booker Prize studied science at university. From there he went to work as an advertising copywriter. The man who wrote *Bliss*, *Oscar and Lucinda* and *True History of the Kelly Gang* also wrote 'You make us smile, Dr Lindeman . . .'

A shining example of the career path well travelled is renowned Olympic hockey coach Ric Charlesworth. Recognised as one of the best sports coaches in the world after taking the Australian women's team to consecutive gold medals, Charlesworth was a first-class player at both hockey and cricket. A veteran of 227 matches for Australia (130 as captain), he was voted Australia's best male hockey player of the century. He also played cricket for Western Australia in the world's top domestic competition, the Sheffield Shield. But for all his talent as a player and his experience of playing sport at the highest level, it was what Charlesworth learnt off the field that he believes helped him become a world-renowned sports coach. Interviewed for this book, Charlesworth said it was what he learnt in his professional life as a doctor and later as a member of parliament that gave him the skills needed for his new career path.

I learnt more about teamwork as a doctor than I ever did as an athlete. To see a surgical team in action – a whole range of people working together, often under extreme time pressures – is to see a team working in perfect harmony. In a typical ward you saw doctors, orderlies, nursing staff, pharmacists, physiotherapists, occupational therapists, catering staff – you name it – all working towards providing patient care. The doctors controlled critical technical areas, but it was the nursing staff who made it all happen. They were the glue that held everything together and that is so similar to the situation you have in a sporting team. Certain people think they are in charge, but it takes the efforts of a whole range of people if the team is to succeed.

So much of what I learnt in my training as a doctor was applicable to my career as a coach: from attitudes to the practical approach. The surgeons who taught us as students instilled things like diligence, attention to detail and the need for preparation. All those things I was able to use in my coaching. Then, there were the actual skills I acquired as a doctor that I could use directly. I knew about physiology and psychology. Counselling a player is not that different to counselling a patient. I was also able to challenge the medical staff. If they said a player was suffering a certain injury, I was qualified to question that opinion if I felt it needed challenging.

And how did ten years as a member of Federal parliament help him as a coach? 'I saw the opposite of teamwork in action on occasions and learned to listen to both sides of an argument,' he said. No doubt he also learnt not to take too much notice of what is written in the newspapers.

Ric Charlesworth decided to leave medicine and stand for public office due to his disenchantment with the inequalities of Australia's social system. His work as a locum visiting homes in disadvantaged areas spurred him to change his career and move into politics, where he felt he could make a difference. He had also reached the stage where he did not want to continue in private practice. 'The alternatives were further specialisation or a change in direction,' he said.

It was the dilemma that literally thousands of people face every day: to stay in a job in which they do not feel fulfilled or to move on. Charlesworth chose the latter, standing for a seat in parliament. However, after a decade as a backbencher, with his Party in Opposition and his family suffering from his long absences, he retired from public office and took up his first coaching position.

'I was in a safe seat and thought I would get to the front bench eventually,' he said. 'But the price was just too high. My children were growing up without me and if I had risen further up the political ladder the situation with my family would only have worsened. I never regretted the decision to leave the job. In fact, there was a real feeling of freedom in the release.'

Of course not all of us are as fortunate as Ric Charlesworth, who had a dream job waiting in the wings. The decision to leave the security of a job (no matter how far short that job falls of your perception of a 'dream' job) is never taken easily.

## STAGES IN THE WORK CYCLE

It could be said that people go through a cycle of four stages in the course of their working lives. The first stage is one of confident incompetence. This is when the employee first starts a job and has yet to master its intricacies. They might not yet be good at the job, but they have high levels of motivation. Everything is new and exciting. They want to do well and are willing to work hard to achieve that goal.

In the next stage of the cycle, the worker's competence grows but their motivation wavers. They experience huge highs and lows. They are starting to have doubts. They can do the job, but they are starting to look around them. Is it really possible to get to the level to which they aspire? Are their workmates really as witty and sophisticated as they first thought? A day later, the motivation may return. Yes, the job is everything that they had hoped and the goal is achievable.

In the third stage, the competence level has evened out and there is a big dip in motivation. The work holds no challenge, the people have lost their mystique. What was once challenging, exciting new territory now holds as much mystery and promise as a movie you have seen ten times.

The fourth stage is the most desirable. It is when competence is high and motivation is high. Everything is working, everything clicks. You know you are in the perfect job. There is enough challenge to keep things interesting, you feel comfortable in your working environment and you can't wait to get into work each morning.

How long do these stages last? That all depends on the person and the job. You could find yourself going through them all within the first year of a job. The last stage, the one that everyone hopes for, could last for four months or 20 years. If it is four months and you fall back to one of the less desirable cycles, it is crunch time. You have a major decision to make.

### The Four Stages of the Work Cycle

Stage 1: Incompetent but confident of gaining mastery/ high motivation
Stage 2: Competence grows/motivation wavers
Stage 3: Competence evens out/motivation dips
Stage 4: Competence high/motivation high

## TIME FOR A CHANGE?

The usual time for change is in stage three, when competence has reached a plateau and motivation is low. People usually become bored when they have totally mastered their work and it no longer holds a challenge for them. This is when they stop being valuable employees. Their energies are no longer concentrated on the job. They may become antisocial, gossipy or office troublemakers. At this stage they should look at their options. They can either seek promotion, transfer to a different job within the organisation, expand the responsibilities of their present job, or leave the company. As we said earlier, they must look at their value system and ask themselves: What is important to me? What motivates me? Is it making money, meeting a challenge, doing something good for others? Whatever it is, that is what they should aim for and that is the goal they should drive their efforts towards. It is crucial to find what interests you, what motivates you, and then take aim in that direction.

Easier said than done, you say? Perhaps, but a good place to start is to look at yourself and the job that is currently falling short of providing you with the motivation you need. Ask yourself, what do you need to learn – even if you don't like it! What is it about your job that you do not like? Is it the actual work, the location, the work environment, the people, the culture or the industry? Whatever it is, isolate that feature of the job and start drilling. A good analogy is peeling back the layers of an onion. You may have a general distaste for part of your job, but when you peel back the various layers you might find that the offending area is only a very small part of the whole. You might say to yourself 'I like everything about my job but . . .' The 'but' could be that you hate writing reports or talking to people. You could be a lawyer who likes talking to people but doesn't like poring over contracts. You might be an accountant who likes people, but doesn't like sitting inside an office working with numbers all day. The point is to isolate what you like and dislike about your current job, because, once you build a picture of the type of job that will excite you, you are in a position to go out and get it.

If you are that hotshot salesperson who likes people but doesn't like cold calling, you should be working in account management where you can look after 'warm' relationships rather than opening new accounts. If you are the accountant who doesn't like being cooped up in an office all day, perhaps you should be looking at a career in sales or personal financial planning that involves visiting customers.

Maybe the key factor in your dissatisfaction doesn't have anything to do with you. It could be the culture of your workplace that is presenting the problem. Maybe you work for a large organisation and have become disenchanted by the lack of input you have. If so, it could be time to join a smaller company or even start your own small business. A key point to remember is that the culture of an organisation is defined by the leadership and the people who work there. For you to be happy, you should work with like-minded people. You should also be doing something you not only like doing, but are good at and that naturally leads to your next career goal. Usually ability and achievement are closely connected and we tend to excel at what we enjoy doing and that leads us forward.

## PREPARING FOR CHANGE

Once you have isolated the pluses and minuses, it is time to start looking around and dipping your toe in the water. The first step is to go through the classified advertisements in print or online in your city's major newspapers. If you are open to the possibility of relocation, order the newspapers from cities that interest you if you can't access them online. Read through every ad and identify the ones you are interested in – irrespective of whether or not you are qualified for the job. You won't be applying for them all, just identifying a pattern and seeing what is out there.

After a month or so of reading the ads, you should have a better picture of the industries – not the specific jobs – that you are interested in pursuing. Simultaneously go to major employment web sites, such as those listed in the 'Further reading' section (pp. 280–2). Type in the industry or profession you are interested in and all jobs listed online from around the world will be revealed.

At the same time, start talking to people, networking with family and friends. As we will explore in the next chapter, even just talking about change puts you in a different mind-set. What was once simply a vague feeling of dissatisfaction has suddenly been transformed into action. You are actually doing something about your situation and that is empowering. If you are particularly interested in a certain activity, join a club and talk to the people you meet there. They will be like-minded people. They will probably be doing the sort of work that would interest you. They might even suggest jobs that you didn't know existed, but which are perfect for your particular skills. With luck you will hear the words: 'Well, I don't think you would like to do what I do, but there is a job in my industry which would be perfect for you.' That is what it is all about: finding a perfect match for your particular skills, your value system and your personality. Don't expect it to present itself overnight – something as valuable as a dream job will take some finding – but follow the steps and you will be surprised at what you discover.

Getting a clear idea as to what you dislike about your present position helps you to determine what you do like and what you are good at, and this knowledge enables you to draw a picture of the type of job that would interest you. Having got to this stage, you can now begin to research what jobs are available that tap your particular skills, strengths and interests. The next step is to write a resumé that targets that specific job. Throwing handfuls of bread on top of the water is fine if you want to watch fish have a nibble and swim away, but landing a certain type of fish requires a certain kind of bait. Your resumé should be aimed specifically at the person you intend to read it. It doesn't have to be overly creative, just effective. Chapter 6, 'Tools for opening the door', goes into detail about resumés.

Finally, get in touch with some experts. All major recruitment firms have specialist consultants who deal with specific industries. They won't be hard to find, just go back to those newspaper advertisements that you have been collecting. The same names will appear time and time again beneath the ads that are of most interest to you.

And don't be afraid to make the move from one job to another. There is no stigma attached to this practice, no perception that a person who moves around is unstable or unemployable. Regardless of how much of a dream job your present unsatisfactory job may have seemed when you started it, chances are it has taken you as far as you can go with it. You have got to the top of the escalator, so it's time to hop on the next one. It happens to nearly everyone, no matter how highly qualified, or how perfect the job might appear. It even happened to Ric Charlesworth who, having made his women's hockey team arguably the most successful sporting team Australia has ever produced, walked away. Why? Because he needed another challenge. He is now involved with an Australian Football League team which finished last in his first year. To some, that might seem a downward step, a ride on the wrong escalator. To Ric Charlesworth, the man to whom it matters most, it is a challenge and that makes it his dream job.

## CASE STUDY
### Doctor to Sportswriter: Doug, 43

When he left school with high marks in 1975, Doug was advised by parents and school counsellors to apply to study medicine at university. An easygoing sporty teenager, he was interested in marine biology and, since both his parents were teachers, he thought teaching might be an option as well.

'Everyone told me it would be better to study a hard-to-get-into course like medicine and then, if I didn't like it, drop down to an easier course like teaching, rather than trying to do it the other way around,' he said.

Doug studied medicine from 1976 to 1981 and graduated with

a Bachelor of Medicine and Surgery. He then began his two-year hospital internship and residency. It was during this period that Doug became disenchanted with his medical career.

I didn't like the hours or the set-up in the public hospital system. There were both internal and external politics. Internally the hierarchy of the hospital was very political and externally the public hospital system was a political football. There was never enough funding. When I was working in the casualty section we had to turn people away on Saturday nights. The hospital was literally full-up. There were times when we had patients who had suffered heart-attacks lying in corridors for four or five hours before we could find them a bed in a ward.

After travelling overseas for a year, Doug returned and did some locum work for local general practitioners. It was then that he admitted to himself that he was not suited to medicine.

I just found it very boring and depressing. A GP listens to people complaining all day. They are right to complain, they are sick, but it just wasn't the job for me. The alternative to general practice was specialising, which meant another five to ten years in the hospital system and I wasn't prepared to do that. To be fair, it wasn't just the system's fault. The fact is that I had gone down the wrong career path.

As he had no financial or emotional commitments, but still harboured a passion for sport, Doug decided to try to make sports reporting his livelihood.

'My father had taught one of our better-known sports commentators years earlier and he put me in touch with him. This man suggested I get some voice training and try to get a job in radio,' he said.

Doug paid for a course at a TV and radio school and managed to get some casual reporting shifts on city and country radio. In 1985 he answered an advertisement calling for reporters for a new specialist sports magazine. Though it was short-lived, the magazine introduced him to established sportswriters. One suggested he write to all major newspapers offering his services and one gave him a job as a sub-editor, editing sports results and reporters' stories. Some 16 years later, Doug is still with the newspaper, as a sportswriter, but says it took some time to overcome his colleagues' misgivings.

I really wanted to be a writer and the fact that I had qualified as a doctor was a big disadvantage. People didn't take me seriously and weren't prepared to give me a chance to write. The feeling was that I was going to be around for only a few months because I was really a doctor trying something different as a bit of a joke. People have a certain image of doctors earning huge money and living a life of luxury. The people at the newspaper couldn't believe I would give that up to be a reporter.

What they didn't realise was that I wasn't interested in the money, I was interested in the satisfaction which comes from doing something I enjoyed. Besides, I really don't think I earn a great deal less than a general practitioner and I certainly don't have to work the long hours or suffer the incredible stress and responsibility that they do.

I have a friend who is an orthopaedic surgeon. I assist him in surgery one day a fortnight and sometimes my wife and I go to his magnificent home. When I see the way he lives I sometimes think that could be me, but just as quickly I think I could never do it. This fellow is probably 99 per cent happy with what he does, which is great. It is just not right for me. I don't know if I have achieved my dream career yet, but I am

certain that I would be a much different person if I was
working as a doctor. I would be grumpier, more irritable.

So if he hasn't found his dream career, where does he think he will
go next?

'It is hard to say,' he said. 'One thing I have found as a sportswriter is
that the pleasure of watching sport has changed for me. There is a huge
difference between doing something because you want to and doing it
because you are paid to.'

Doug gave the example of watching a team he covered playing in the
game that could have earned them a spot in the national grand final or
ended their season. It all came down to one kick at the goal and while
50 000 people in the stadium and millions more watching on television
held their breath, Doug found himself torn.

On the one hand I was thinking, if he kicks this it will be great
for the city and the team, and on the other, if he kicks this
I am going to have a very hard week's work ahead of me.
That is why I wonder if doing something you love for a living
is really possible. I love to go fishing. If I catch something, great.
If I don't, I've still had an enjoyable day, but would I be happy
as a professional fisherman where my livelihood depended
on what I caught? I loved building a carport at my home,
but would I love having to build 100 or 200 carports?

I think maybe the key is trying to do for a living what you
would like to be doing for free and then just letting it take
you wherever it goes. It is all about satisfaction. If at the end
of the day you feel satisfied with what you are doing, that is
as good an outcome as you can hope for.

# 2
# it's all in the mind

One of the greatest stumbling blocks to a person achieving their dream career is often their own self-perception. Often we stay on a career path that no longer suits nor stimulates us simply because we feel unqualified to try anything different. How many times have we all heard the workplace complaint: 'I have been pigeon-holed' or 'I'm in a rut'? Plenty. But how rarely do we hear: 'I have pigeon-holed myself' or 'I have dug myself into a rut'. Yet often we are, at least in part, responsible for putting limitations on our position.

For instance, we tend to label ourselves and think of ourselves as a 'something' rather than as an amalgam of many things. Someone who has trained and worked for years as, say, a teacher, thinks of themselves as just that, 'a teacher' – rather than as a person who is experienced in all the many and varied skills which make up that profession. A nurse might think of herself as 'a nurse' rather than as a person who is experienced at performing numerous sensitive tasks that involve people and doing so under extreme pressure. And, perhaps most common of all, a mother based at home will think of herself as 'a housewife' rather than as someone who has so much to offer any number of employers in a vast range of workplace environments: that is, as a person who can manage many tasks at once, keep calm in stressful situations and manage the busy schedules of a whole team of people who often have conflicting agendas.

## SELF-EVALUATION AND CAREER REALIGNMENT

This natural tendency to mentally pigeon-hole is one of the reasons psychologists play such a major role in the process of career realignment. In our company we employ many psychologists whose major role is to help our clients see what they are capable of and match them with an employer who can best use those particular skills. The psychologist assists in this process of seeing a person stripped of the pigeon-holing labels they normally apply to themselves by, in a sense, holding up a mirror so that the person can see themself, their skills and interests more clearly.

Self-evaluation is critical when we are going through the process of trying to change our lives. However, being totally honest about ourselves is a skill not many of us possess. And even though we all have private dreams and thoughts, all too often they remain just that – dreams and thoughts – rather than actions in reality. It is said that the only thing we have total control over is our own thoughts. To be able to control them – rather than allowing them to control us – we have to get them out into the open. Anyone who is changing jobs needs someone with whom they can externalise issues, bringing them to the surface and acknowledging their presence. That is where a psychologist comes into the picture. Psychologists are very good at asking the right questions and probing to get the answers that will unlock the door to a new career.

'Once a thought is verbalised it registers in a different part of the brain,' explains one of our psychologists. When something is actually spoken out loud and shared with someone, it can be, psychologically speaking, externalised and objectified. In other words, it is taken out of that musty cabinet drawer where we store our most secret dreams and aspirations, brushed off, looked at and eventually acted upon.

Many people don't really know what they want. They can't easily find something to give them the motivation needed to push their buttons and, in turn, achieve their dream career. Sometimes an employment psychologist can help them to identify interests and find their path. The process might start with a few easy questions such as: What are you good at? What do you like doing?

Our psychologists have several psychological assessment tests to draw upon. Some are very simple, others are clinical psychological tools. All are used to provide a profile and paint a picture of who the client really is. Sometimes the portrait will resemble someone the client knows very well. Sometimes it will present them with a stranger. But in reality, it is a portrait of who they actually are.

Psychologists help people to be objective, as one of ours explains:

It might be a case of taking someone to the next step in their thought process. When I'm talking to a client I will ask them about themselves. They might say: 'I'm good with people.' Some people might just accept that statement and move on, but a psychologist will probe further and ask them 'Why?' Why do they consider themselves to be good with people and in what areas? It is surprising how often people have a perception about themselves, but never really break it down or examine it closely. When they ask themselves what it is that makes them good with people or what it is that they like about people, they might find that they are good at selling an idea to people, or good at understanding what others are saying. They might have a natural ability to nurture and offer support. All this is vital information. It helps us to put together a clearer profile that we can then better match to an employer. In turn, it helps the person better understand themself and to know what it is that they can do and do well.

Often, when a client is encouraged to look within, they will paint a profile of a person that does not fit in with where they have spent their working lives. It is then that the psychologist can start mapping out a new path to get that person to a place where their hidden skills can be used. In a sense, the psychologist gives the person permission to be themself.

Of course it is not always that easy. Sometimes the person does not want to accept, or even believe, that the profile we have uncovered from the questions and psychological tests is really who they are. As a career psychologist explains:

Most people are not good at self-examination, which is why they come to us. They want to move, they need to talk, and we have an idea of the market. They think it will be a case of coming to us, telling us what they see as their dream job and asking us to line up some interviews. Sometimes we have to be honest and tell people they are not suited to what they see as their dream. They may come to us and tell us that they want to apply for senior appointments and we have to tell them that their psychological profile shows that they are not decisive. They are not good in controlling positions,

31

but are more suited to consultative roles. We have to reflect the truth and sometimes play the devil's advocate. Often these people have never had anyone to bounce these sorts of ideas around with before and reflect back to them what their deepest interests and values actually are, in spite of their preconceptions about themselves. They don't always like it, because they may not be used to honesty. They want to match themselves with their earliest notion of success. They think in order to achieve it they have to be at the very top of an organisation. The truth is career paths are no longer always vertical. They can move horizontally or zigzag. A person might be much better off – happier and more fulfilled – moving right to left or left to right, rather than bottom to top.

## ONWARDS AND UPWARDS OR ZIGZAG?

The deep-seated belief that a career path has to be an upward climb, rather than a move sideways or even initially backwards to achieve the right result is a hard one to shake. Our psychologist explains:

In our society the perception of a good job is management, because the concept of being 'in charge' is a positive one. A lot of people think being the boss is about sitting in a nice office and telling people what to do. But leadership is a tough job. Sometimes being 'in charge' is not the right match for a job seeker. Sometimes a dream job is not the one that gives you the most responsibility, but the one that enables you to maximise your skills. That might be as middle management, or working on your own as a salesperson.

Our dream job might even be waiting to be found in an area totally removed from our first foray into the work force. Our earliest dream is not necessarily the one that is guaranteed to make us happy. There is a perception that the child who wanted to be a fireman and achieved that has succeeded. That is not always the case. There are plenty of disenchanted doctors out there. They went through their training expecting a certain thing and found themselves running a business in an entirely different environment. There are general practitioners who are upset that they were not able to become specialists or researchers. The fact is that there is often a big difference between the perception of success and the reality.

There is a school of thought that we should not limit ourselves to our perception of the ideal. Noted British psychologist Karen Horny has expressed her theory that the more we move towards our ideal self, the more life passes us by. If we move along a narrow path, allowing ourselves only those experiences that fit in with our image of who we want to be, we cut ourselves off from things on the sides of the path. We say we won't read that book or see that movie because it is not 'our kind' of book or movie. We become closed off to other experiences for which we might be better suited. It is the same when striving for the dream job. Those people with broader aspirations, who look outside the square, are more self-actualised. They are happier with the way they are, learning more along the way and enjoying what's on offer.

Be careful what you wish for, as you might get something quite different from what you thought you wanted. Also be wary of biting off more than you can handle in a job. The truth is that a one-size-fits-all ideal does not exist. What is ideal for one person is not ideal for another. What a married man with a wife, three children and a paid-off home will think of as a perfect job will be entirely different from the ideal job for a single mum with three kids and a mortgage. Because of this the ideal job makes a value statement. If you are looking for status and feel that a Porsche and membership of an exclusive golf club will give it to you, great. However, if you want security for yourself and your family and two weeks at the beach each Christmas, that is fine too.

## TO CHANGE OR NOT TO CHANGE?

Often people want to change, but don't know why. Sometimes the best job seekers don't know what they want or can even hope to do. They might have been working in one area for so long that the idea of change is daunting. They realise that they need a change, but have become so set in their ways that it remains unclear what direction they should turn in order to make that change. Or they may have been out of the work force for so long that they don't realise how much is open to them. Sound familiar? We have just described the traditional husband and at-home wife scenarios.

Generally speaking, men change direction more rarely because they have developed 'tunnel vision' and, as the breadwinner with a family dependent on them, can't so easily take career risks. Men tend to have one focus, whereas women are more adaptable and more able to manage more than one thing at a time. A man is more likely to set a certain work orientation and direction early on. Usually the goal is simple: get to the top – even if it is not what he really wants. He will be concentrating on making a living and supporting a family.

Meanwhile, his wife has been running the household, catering to the needs of the children and juggling a hundred things at once. When the children are older, she may consider re-entering the work force. As a potential employee she is likely to be more adaptable, more open to change and more willing to consider a wide range of options. And why shouldn't she be? During the period when women are child-rearing, they have had to re-invent themselves. They may have given up a job, had children, raised the children, said goodbye to the children. Over that period they have remade themselves, and had plenty of time to think about what they are going to do when the children grow up. The fact is that they have been acquiring skills that can be very sought-after. It is just that they do not think of them as skills, rather as part of the many chores that keep their household running smoothly.

Smart countries encourage women with families to enter and re-enter the work force. Why wouldn't they try to encourage a large percentage of the educated population to contribute to society and the country's economic productivity! This also leads to the debate about paid maternity leave, which really strikes at the heart of society viewing 'work' in a different way.

## SKILL SET VERSUS JOB LABEL

Employees who have been working in one industry for a long period of time may find themselves in a similar position to the housewife. They may feel stuck with a label that no longer fits comfortably. Let's go back to the example of the nurse. Ask a nurse to describe themself and, they are likely to say they have three certificates and are qualified to work in a hospital. A more objective assessment by an employment psychologist analysing skill sets and knowledge would say that this person has experience working with a small team, staying in control during crises, calming anxious and agitated people, using available information to answer queries, and working long hours. A nurse also pays great attention to detail, knows how to operate high-tech apparatus and has first-hand knowledge of the health system. The nurse's own description would suit an employer looking to hire a nurse. The psychologist would open up any number of possibilities for the person who no longer wants to go on nursing. That person might end up as a tour guide, they could be involved in client service or in the sale of medical equipment or pharmaceuticals. They could use their knowledge to work in the health insurance industry or employ their skills to manage a sales team. Suddenly we are looking at a much wider range of possibilities.

A session or two with a career-adviser psychologist will show a person not only that they have hidden skills, but also that they have skills that will enable them to change direction. Skills used in one career path are often transferable to a different career. A job seeker should look at their skills as part of a package of assets that will help them get to where they really want to be, rather than as a ball and chain tying them down and keeping them where they are. Once someone has that knowledge and enlightened self-perception, they are in a position to move. And when they are asked about themselves, they will be able to say much more and convey more useful information. After all, an employer doesn't just want to know what a prospective employee has done, they want to know what they can do.

The ability to communicate your range of skills, rather than simply list your previous job experience is one of the most important elements in changing career paths. And, sadly, it is often lacking. Think about it: if you were asked in an interview situation to describe yourself, would you say something like, 'I am decisive, I am a team player, but I am not afraid to make the hard decisions' or 'Well, for the past fourteen years I have been administration manager at XYZ Pty Ltd. Before that I did a three-year cadetship at PQR Corporation while I was studying for my BA'?

It is very common for people to respond to the question 'Tell me a little bit about yourself' with a job-by-job description of what they have done. They don't usually look at what they can do and put it together into a package that can then be marketed.

The role of the recruiter or psychologist is to help the client think objectively about their real self and promote that self into a work environment.

One of our counsellors explains.

Put simply, people don't tell stories well and an interesting story is exactly what the interviewers want. If they are after a list of previous positions, they will look at a resumé. What they want to hear is the person in front of them telling the story between the lines of the resumé. The job of the psychologist is to help the job seeker relate to what the employer wants to hear.

And while the idea of going to a psychologist might sound threatening to some people, in this context, it is more a matter of the counsellor or psychologist helping the job seeker to better market themself and adopt the mindset of the employer.

The employer is buying a concept. He or she wants to know what the job seeker can do, rather than what he or she has done. A lot of people say where they have been, not where they can go, given the opportunity. People have to be objective. They have to deliver just to get into the interview in the first place, and then they have to deliver comparatively to get the job.

## COMMUNICATION SKILLS FOR SUCCESS

Whether or not that happens can come down to communication skills. Coaching a job seeker on how to speak to the interviewer is another area in which a psychologist can make an enormous difference. A common problem occurs when the job seeker assumes that the interviewer knows as much as the job seeker knows.

People who have worked for a long time in one industry or marketplace will unconsciously pick up the terminology of that industry and, having spoken this industry lingo to their colleagues for so long, will tend to forget that not everyone speaks this way. An example is someone who has worked for a long period in the public service speaking in acronyms and terms not generally used outside the public service.

Another part of the psychologist's job is to unlock the client's thought process by helping them understand simple psychology. A lot of people in the interview situation think if they are pleasant and can make the interviewer smile or laugh at a joke and generally like them, they are bound to get the job. In reality, this is not the case. The interviewer isn't looking for a new pal, he or she is looking for someone who has what it takes to perfectly fill the role on offer. The psychologist can coach the job seeker about how to convey more than that they are a nice person and therefore can do the job. The job seeker must validate themselves by saying things in the interview that can be objectively assessed.

Another issue relates to what type of person you naturally are. Our psychologist gives this example.

Often we will see people who are clever and have a great deal to offer an employer, but do not have the persona to promote themselves. These are what are called Beta types. That is, they are quiet and intelligent. They have questioning minds and can approach problems from a different way to most people. They see things objectively and critically. Often they are the type of people who will sit in a meeting without saying a word – until the very end, when they will come up with a clever comment or solution that shows they have not only been paying attention, but in fact have been way ahead of everyone else. These people rarely contribute to group discussions and for that matter are often left behind in a corporate environment while other less intelligent colleagues advance.

An array of psychological assessments can help people to understand themselves better. Telling people what 'type' they are gives them permission to be that sort of person and often can show them a way to advance within an organisation or point out a different path they should be taking. Psychological assessment is all about unlocking what is inside, seeing what is there and then working with it to the best advantage.

## CASE STUDY
## From Middle Management to Psychologist:
## Anne, aged 50-something

Anne left school at the age of fifteen, but had always harboured a desire to study at tertiary level. At the age of 44 – having worked for the past twelve years for a consumer goods firm and rising to middle management – she decided to follow her dream. With the support of her husband, Anne enrolled in a twelve-month preparatory course with the University of Sydney. At the end of the course she sat the university entrance exam and was accepted into a Bachelor of Arts course, majoring in psychology. After studying full-time for three years, Anne graduated with her degree. Then came the hard part: finding a job that offered an opportunity to utilise both her commercial experience and her newly attained academic qualifications.

'I applied to various organisations on the open market and did not score any interviews,' Anne said. 'So I proceeded to cold-call companies and was given a chance by an organisation specialising in out-placement and helping clients with career transition.'

It proved to be an excellent fit. Anne's work entails helping people who have been retrenched to cope with the emotional stress of job loss and to set about equipping themselves to re-enter the work force. With her background as a long-time employee who retrained and made a successful career change at a time when many people would have thought their options were limited, she is able to relate to her clients' situations. She has also worked as a counsellor with the Alzheimer's Association.

With her new career being everything she had hoped for and more, Anne is embarking on further studies to upgrade her qualifications.

I am currently doing a part-time postgraduate university course to gain full membership of the New South Wales Psychology Board as a psychologist. At the age of 50-plus I have embarked on a totally new career that is both fascinating and rewarding.

When I was studying I really thought that I would never get paid work and would have to work only in volunteer roles, but the way things have turned out has more than justified the time and effort I put in. I have been lucky to have had great support from my family, especially my husband, and I can honestly say that going to university and now using my degree to help others is a dream come true.

# 3
# mind games

The tests psychologists use to help a person through the process of career change fulfil a number of aims. Their results help determine which 'type' a person is, and can suggest a range of jobs best suited to their particular personality and temperament. The tests might also assess a person's 'career drivers' – that is, the inner forces that determine what a person wants and needs from their working life. Or they may be aimed simply at getting you to think about where you are in your career and therefore provide a catalyst for change.

In this chapter we will give examples of some psychological tests and also present some of the quizzes that appear on career portal Monster.com. In all these examples, there is no right or wrong answer (although the on-line quizzes will provide a 'result'). Rather the questions that follow should be answered as an exercise to provide experience in two of the most important elements of change: the ability to answer questions with insight and honesty, and the ability to look at oneself objectively. The psychological tests provide an understanding of inner-self or type:

the compass that points us in the direction of the right career. The quizzes, some more serious than others, are tools for self-analysis – a way to get used to thinking about what you are doing in your working life and how you are doing it. Like most things in life, self-analysis is something that must be practised and perfected. Responding to something as seemingly inconsequential as an 'Are you really happy?' quiz in a magazine or newspaper could be a first step towards finding the key that unlocks a whole new understanding of yourself and your place in the world.

One of the best and most effective series of psychological tests to help with the process of career change are those owned by Richard L. Knowdell, whose materials are supplied in Australasia by Worklife Pty Ltd in Sydney. Three that are particularly helpful are the Career Drivers Survey, Personal Skills Matrix and Values Card Sort. As their titles suggest, these tests determine the elements that drive a career, classify and prioritise what is most valuable to a person in terms of work values, and identify skill strengths. Importantly, as was mentioned in the previous chapter, the 'Personal Skills Matrix' also identifies skills that can be transferred to other careers or career paths. While these tests take some time to complete and assess, a brief run-down of each gives insight into the type of tests that will be encountered in the process of career change, and the skills required to complete them to best advantage.

## CAREER DRIVERS SURVEY

The Career Drivers Survey helps uncover the consistent themes that shape and guide life and work decisions. It consists of 36 pairs of statements. The person completing the survey must evaluate the relative importance of each statement and allocate a total of three points between the pair. For instance, in one pair of statements, the person might find one statement overwhelmingly important and the other not important at all, therefore the points would be allocated 3–0. Other pairs could be much closer in importance, perhaps even seemingly impossible to choose between. This would result in a 2–1 or 1–2 score.

Pairs of statements that must be given a relative value include:

- I will only be satisfied with an unusually high standard of living; **or**, I wish to have considerable influence over other people.
- I only feel satisfied if the output from my job has real value in itself; **or**, I want to be an expert in the things I do.
- I enjoy feeling that people look up to me; **or**, Not to put too fine a point on it, I want to be wealthy.
- My work is part of my search for meaning in life; **or**, I want the things that I produce to bear my name.
- I seek to be able to afford anything I want; **or**, A job with long-term security really appeals to me.
- Frankly, I want to tell other people what to do; **or**, For me, being close to others is really the important thing.
- At the end of the day, I do what I believe is important, not what simply promotes my career; **or**, I seek public recognition.

The numbers scored for each of the 72 statements are recorded, which enables a graph to be drawn that maps the importance of personal career drivers in nine distinct categories:

- *Material Rewards:* seeking possessions, wealth and a high standard of living
- *Power/Influence:* seeking to be in control of people and resources
- *Search for Meaning:* seeking to do things that are believed to be valuable for their own sake
- *Expertise:* seeking a high level of accomplishment in a specialised field

- *Creativity:* seeking to innovate and be identified with original output
- *Affiliation:* seeking supportive relationships with others at work
- *Autonomy:* seeking to be independent and able to make key decisions for oneself
- *Security:* seeking a solid and predictable future
- *Status:* seeking to be recognised, admired and respected by the community at large.

## PERSONAL SKILLS MATRIX

The Personal Skills Matrix is a chart and series of questions that entails the person objectively listing their skills and rating them in terms of proficiency and enjoyment of use. This is a way to identify and confirm skill strengths and preferences, while also identifying transferable skills and those skills that have been learned not just as a result of formal education and training but also through work and life experience. This test:

- confirms significant patterns, identifying the set of skills that may be used in a number of different occupations
- highlights areas of proficiency and enjoyment that could be used as building blocks for an alternative career
- reinforces knowledge of skills that should be promoted in resumés and interviews.

## VALUES CARD SORT

The Values Card Sort is aimed at identifying, classifying and prioritising an individual's work values. A series of cards listing possible attributes and benefits of a job (such as quick advancement, high status, power to make decisions or be of service to others) are sorted into the categories Always Valued, Often Valued, Sometimes Valued, Seldom Valued or Never Valued. The top seven cards in the Always Valued category are then placed in order of priority and expanded upon, thus adding further to the profile or picture the career psychologist is able to paint. Additionally, just the simple fact of engaging in the process of considering and answering these questions, takes a person further along the path of self-analysis, which is a vital ingredient of change.

## MYERS BRIGGS TYPE INDICATOR

Another psychological test much valued by employment professionals is the Myers Briggs Type Indicator (MBTI). A simple test based on the work of Swiss psychologist Carl Jung and two Americans, Katharine Briggs and Isabel Briggs Myers, it is used to determine personality type. Once that type has been determined, it can be related to a range of most suitable careers. To take this test, read the descriptions of the four dimensions or aspects of type below, and choose which characteristics in each pair describe you best (for example, Extrovert or Introvert). Your personality type is made up of your natural preference for each of these four dimensions.

### MYERS BRIGGS TYPE INDICATOR

1. *Where is your energy naturally directed?*
Extroverts' energy is directed primarily outward towards people and things outside of themselves. Introverts' energy is primarily directed inward towards their own thoughts, perceptions and reactions. Therefore, Extroverts tend to be more naturally active, expressive, social and interested in many things, whereas Introverts tend to be more reserved, private, cautious and interested in fewer interactions, but with greater depth and focus.

### Extroverts (E) often:
- have high energy
- talk a lot

- think out loud
- like to be around people a lot
- are easily distracted.

**Introverts (I) often:**

- have quiet energy
- talk less
- think before they act
- are comfortable spending time alone
- have good concentration.

**Choose Extrovert (E) or Introvert (I).**

**2.  What kind of information do you naturally notice and remember?**
Sensors notice the facts, details and realities of the world around them, whereas Intuitives are more interested in connections and relationships between facts, as well as the meaning or possibilities of the information. Sensors tend to be practical and literal people who trust their past experience and often have good common sense. Intuitives tend to be imaginative, theoretical people who trust their hunches and pride themselves on their creativity.

**Sensors (S) often:**

- admire practicality
- focus on the facts and specifics
- have straightforward speech
- are more realistic, see what is
- are more present-oriented.

**Intuitives (N) often:**

- admire creativity
- focus on ideas and the big picture
- have roundabout thoughts
- are more imaginative, see possibilities
- are more future-oriented.

**Choose Sensor (S) or Intuitive (N).**

### 3. *How do you decide or come to conclusions?*

Thinkers make decisions based primarily on objective and impersonal criteria: what makes the most sense and what is logical. Feelers make decisions based primarily on their personal values and how they feel about the choices. So, Thinkers tend to be cool, analytical, and are convinced by logical reasoning. Feelers tend to be sensitive, empathetic, and are compelled by extenuating circumstances and a constant search for harmony.

#### *Thinkers (T) often:*

- are cool and reserved
- are objective
- are honest and direct
- are naturally critical
- are motivated by achievement.

#### *Feelers (F) often:*

- are warm and friendly
- get their feelings hurt easily
- are sensitive and diplomatic
- try hard to please others
- are motivated by being appreciated.

#### **Choose Thinker (T) or Feeler (F).**

### 4. *What kind of environment makes you the most comfortable?*

Judgers prefer a structured, ordered and fairly predictable environment, where they can make decisions and have things settled. Perceivers prefer to experience as much of the world as possible, so they like to keep their options open and are most comfortable adapting. So Judgers tend to be organised and productive, while Perceivers tend to be flexible, curious and nonconforming.

#### *Judgers (J) often:*

- are serious and formal
- are time-conscious

- like to make plans
- work first, play later
- like to finish projects best.

**_Perceivers (P) often:_**

- are playful and casual
- are unaware of time or late
- like to wait-and-see
- play first, work later
- like to start projects best.

**Choose Judger (J) or Perceiver (P).**

Total your results. You should fall into one of two types, either ENFP (Extrovert, Intuitive, Feeler, Perceiver) or ISTJ (Introvert, Sensor, Thinker, Judger).

ENFP's tend to be enthusiastic, talkative and outgoing; clever, curious and playful; deeply caring, sensitive and gentle; highly innovative, creative, optimistic and unique; adaptable and resourceful but sometimes disorganised. The most important thing to ENFPs is the freedom to see possibilities, make connections and be with a variety of people. Popular and often satisfying careers for people whose personality type is ENFP include: advertising account executive, career counsellor, management consultant, developer of educational software, journalist, graphic designer, art director, copywriter, corporate trainer, psychologist, inventor and human resources professional.

ISTJ's tend to be cautious, conservative and quiet; literal, realistic and practical; careful and precise; logical, honest and matter-of-fact; resistant to change and comfortable with routine; hardworking and responsible. The most important thing to ISTJs is being of service, working hard, and being responsible. Popular and often satisfying careers for ISTJs include: chief information officer, meteorologist, database administrator, hospital administrator, paralegal, accountant, real-estate broker, detective, construction/building inspector, physician, office manager and credit analyst.

## SO, WHAT'S YOUR P.Q. (PROMOTABILITY QUOTIENT)?

*The following quiz by Barbara Reinhold appears at content.monster. com.au/tools/quizzes/promotability/. It provides experience in the art of questioning one's position in life, both personally and professionally.*

This quiz presents some dilemmas that people face every day at work. The choices they make in these situations have a tremendous impact on how they are viewed by co-workers and bosses – and hence how promotable they are.

What choices would you make in the following scenarios?

### THE PROMOTABILITY QUOTIENT TEST

1.  *One of your co-workers has just been given the assignment you desperately wanted. You are furious, because you know she got it only because the boss has more than a professional interest in her. What do you do?*

- Tell your co-worker what you think is going on so that she'll turn down the assignment and you can be next in line.
- Quit – you're sick of being undervalued in this company again.
- Prepare your case carefully and go to your boss for a discussion of what you could bring to an assignment like this one. Ask if you could possibly assist on this assignment, in order to be prepared to head up a similar project in the future.

2.  *Your boss seems to have it in for you. You're convinced she watches you more than others in the office and likes to see you fail. How are you going to handle this?*

- Go to Human Resources to find out about filing a grievance. It's always better to respond with strength in situations like this.
- Check with some co-workers. If they agree she treats you differently, meet alone with your boss to ask, in a

non-threatening way, what you could do to enhance your performance, or what it is you have done to displease her.

- Start looking for a new job.

3.  *You're still at work at 6 p.m. on Friday. The project for Monday isn't finished, but you have company arriving for dinner at your house at 7:30 p.m. What do you do?*

- Phone and cancel. It's first things first where you work.
- Explain to your boss that you have guests arriving shortly and must put things on hold, but you'll be in tomorrow to finish.
- Tell your boss about your event, apologise for leaving, and promise to come in over the weekend to finish up. Somewhere in the conversation, however, mention that you'll be thinking of ways for the group to function more efficiently in the future so that projects can be completed on time.

4.  *You're working on a team and sharing your ideas with other people from the department. You're shocked to find that one of your co-workers has taken some of your ideas and is passing them off as his own. What do you do?*

- Confront him immediately in the meeting, so that he knows not to take advantage of you again.
- Confront him after the meeting in private, and make it clear that you won't tolerate his pirating your ideas again.
- Write a letter to the boss calling attention to your co-worker's dishonesty, with a cc to the co-worker.

5.  *At your performance evaluation, your boss suggests that you update your computer skills, particularly those related to the Internet. What do you do?*

- Agree to take on some training whenever your boss sets it up.
- Agree to attend training but, since you're an hourly worker rather

than a salaried employee, only on company time. You're not about to be taken advantage of.

- Look into training options, pick the ones you like best, and discuss them with your boss before getting the training set up.

6. *You're short about three units on your degree, but things are so busy you haven't had time to think about registering this semester at the local college, where you've been enrolled part-time. Today is the last day to sign up. What do you do?*

- Just let it go – the degree doesn't have much relevance to the kind of work you're doing now anyway and you'll make yourself crazy trying to do it all. Life's too short.
- Talk to your boss about finishing your degree. Explain that you may be a little overloaded, but you feel you'll be a better employee in the long run if you take one unit for each of the next three semesters.
- Start back at uni or college, but don't tell anyone – they may take you less seriously if they think you'll get your degree and leave.

7. *It's important to you to do a good job and get things in on time. You're finishing a big assignment two days early and you have some time on your hands. What do you do?*

- Use the time to organise your workspace even more.
- Ask your co-workers if they need some help.
- Let the boss know you're finishing early and ask if there are things she'd like you to do to move other projects along.
- Go find more work or start on the next project.

## DO YOU HAVE WHAT IT TAKES TO BE AN ENTREPRENEUR?

*The following assessment appears at content.monster.com.au/tools/ quizzes/entrepreneur/.*

1. *How do you feel about hard work?*
   - I can't work long hours.
   - I do what the job requires.
   - I have a proven history of being a hard worker.
   - I can work hard if I need to, but would rather not.

2. *How would you describe your energy level?*
   - I'm affected by the moon.
   - I'm indefatigable.
   - I have enough stamina when I need it.
   - I need my time off.

3. *How would you characterise your approach to a new task?*
   - I like to know what the boundaries of the job are.
   - I hate to have someone peering over my shoulder.
   - I prefer to have explicit instructions.
   - I'm a self-starter.

4. *When I step back and think about where I'm going, I realise that:*
   - My most important job is setting meaningful goals.
   - I don't know what 'success' means.
   - I want to make enough money to retire comfortably.
   - I get bored when things go smoothly.

5. *When it comes to risk-taking:*
   - I play the horses.
   - I like the challenge of long odds.
   - I bet on my own skills, not on luck.
   - I think that business is a roll of the dice.

6. *What do you depend on when making assessments?*
   - I'm really smart.

- I follow my hunches.
- I am decisive.
- I'm street-smart.

7. *How does your personality dovetail with your work style?*
- I have to see projects through to their completion.
- Sometimes I drop out.
- I am tenacious, a regular bulldog.
- I'm an easygoing person.

8. *When it comes to looking over my scorecard:*
- I set goals so I can measure my progress.
- I like to see results quickly.
- I welcome constructive criticism.
- Feedback is vitally important to me.

9. *How would you describe your communications skills?*
- I always communicate clearly.
- I sometimes have trouble getting my point across.
- I set the goals; it's up to my employees to achieve them.
- I'm a doer, not a communicator.

10. *How do you deal with the future?*
- I plan ahead. Carefully.
- I don't have a crystal ball, so why waste time planning?
- I try to look ahead.
- Que sera, sera.

11. *When it comes to the type of business you want to start, how much experience have you had?*
- I'm new to this business.
- I know this business from working in it.

- I've been in a similar business, though not the same.
- All businesses are basically the same, so lack of experience is no barrier.

**12.** *How would you describe your attitude towards the group?*
- I am a good employee.
- I am more of a coach than a team player.
- I welcome responsibility.
- I'm a team player.

**13.** *What's your style when things are chaotic or unresolved?*
- I'm a closure person.
- I get stressed if I don't know the answer.
- I can live with incomplete information and uncertainty.
- I can't always wait for complete information before making a decision.

**14.** *Which choice best describes the relationship between your business and your feelings?*
- This business really excites me.
- I see this business as my ticket to riches.
- The more I know about this business, the more I like it.
- There are plenty of exciting businesses. The trick is focusing on one of them.

**15.** *How would you assess your attitude towards financing your venture?*
- I can bootstrap my business.
- I know how to raise money.
- All I need is an income.
- I have a lot of money tucked away for this venture.

**16.** *How do you feel about working with or relying on others?*

- I'm reliable and find others to be the same.
- I'm careful not to go overboard.
- I'm very results-oriented.
- Nice guys finish last.

### 17. *How do you feel when the buck stops with you?*

- I don't make excuses.
- Unfair competition scares me.
- I learn from my mistakes.
- I'd rather be the main player than a support player.

### 18. *How's your self-confidence?*

- I have a 'can do' attitude most of the time.
- I didn't lose. I ran out of time.
- I sometimes wonder if I'm making the right decision.
- Sometimes you win, sometimes you lose.

### 19. *What do you think of creativity and change?*

- I like to follow set patterns.
- Being innovative and creative is a drawback in business.
- I like to come up with new solutions to problems.
- Once my plans are set I never deviate from them.

### 20. *What's your attitude towards sharing your burdens with those close to you?*

- I'm keeping this venture a secret for the time being.
- My friends and family are behind me in this venture.
- My wife is worried about the risk, but we'll work it out.
- I don't know if my friends and family think this is a good idea.

### 21. *How do you feel about 'doing it all'?*

- I have all the business skills I need.

- I'm a people person. What else do I need?
- I don't know what I need to know. Help!
- I have most of the skills and can find people with those I lack.

## ARE YOU READY TO NEGOTIATE YOUR SALARY?
*The following quiz by Michael Chaffers appears at content.monster.com.au/ tools/quizzes/areyouready/.*

Whether you're sitting down with your boss, an HR representative, or someone you want to work for, your ability to get what you want depends on your preparation. So think about what you want, what the other side wants, and how you can persuade him or her to come around to your way of thinking. Preparing for a successful negotiation requires clear thinking, focussed attention and the willingness to do some research. To gauge how well you have prepared and how ready you are to negotiate, answer these questions.

1. *Are you sure you have selected the most appropriate person(s) with whom to negotiate?*
- Yes, I considered all the different people who have influence over my career and some role in deciding its future.
- No, I just assumed that my boss is the right person.
- No, it did not seem worth thinking about.

2. *Have you identified the important issues that you and your company want to negotiate (e.g. salary increase, non-monetary compensation, job responsibilities, etc.)?*
- Yes, I have, and I have also asked my boss about what she expects from me.
- I know I want to talk salary, but I haven't anticipated what my boss wants to discuss.

- I am only interested in the bottom line – how much they are willing to pay me.

3. *For each of the issues above, have you thought about what you really need and why you need it?*
- Yes, I have asked myself why I want what I want and tried to determine what I really care about. Then I prioritised the items on my list.
- No, I have a sense of what is important to me, but I have not really examined why.
- No, I want more money and a promotion.

4. *Have you tried to predict what the company wants out of this negotiation?*
- Yes, I have anticipated what my boss's agenda may be, then consulted with colleagues who've been through similar meetings.
- No, I assume we have the same goals, but I'm not really sure.
- No, I don't see why its agenda is important. I know what I want.

5. *If you do not like what your boss offers you in this meeting, have you considered what you will do?*
- Yes, I have developed a Plan B that includes actions I will take and alternative ideas that will work for both sides.
- No, if I have to, I can think on my feet and adjust my requests to what they offer.
- Yes, if I do not get what I want, I will think hard about leaving.

6. *How would you know if the offer presented to you were fair and appropriate?*
- I have researched the market and my company to find out the typical range of salaries and compensation for people with similar skills and experience.

- I have asked a few of my peers at work what they make.
- If I get what I ask for, then I know it is fair.

7. *Do you know who has the final sign-off on the outcome of your negotiation?*
- Yes, I am aware of the chain of command that is responsible for finalising this process and have thought of ways to help my boss present my case to senior management.
- No, I just figured that my boss would make the decision.
- No, I think my work speaks for itself.

8. *Is there anything about your relationship with your boss that may make this conversation difficult?*
- No, we always discuss any problems as they occur, so I don't foresee having to address them during our meeting.
- Yes, we've had conflicts in the past, and I am prepared to address them if they come up.
- Yes, but if conflicts come up, I will point out that the meeting is about my work performance, not our personal differences.

9. *Have you put together a plan for the meeting?*
- Yes, I have written an agenda to make sure that I touch on all the key issues.
- No, I know what I want to talk about, but I'm not sure what my priorities should be.
- No, I don't think the sequence in which I discuss each issue matters, as long as I know what I want.

## IS SELF-EMPLOYMENT FOR YOU?

*The following quiz by Pat Boer appears at content.monster.com.au/ changers/tools/quizzes/self_employment/.*

Do you envy people who own their own businesses? Dreaming about being self-employed is often the first step to creating a new business or career. If you've been considering self-employment, you need to ask yourself a few key questions before you quit your job. Answer yes to the following questions if applicable.

1. Do you hope to eliminate the negatives of being an employee?
2. Do you have funds to cover expenses for the first few years?
3. Do you need to earn a living during the start-up phase?
4. Can you live without a steady pay cheque?
5. Can you test out the strength of your interest by starting your business part time?
6. Are you specialised in your field?
7. Do you have a written business plan, projecting first-year profits or losses?
8. Can you delay gratification, waiting three to five years for success?
9. Are you well known in your community?
10. Can you control your emotions, accepting business or clients when you're tired?
11. Are you computer literate enough to handle your own billings, taxes, records, etc.?
12. Can you invest in and afford to keep up with technology?
13. Do you have an accountant, solicitor and other professionals to assist your business?
14. Do you have a professional network of supporters to make referrals to your business?
15. Are you self-motivated, with a strong vision and faith in yourself to persevere?
16. Do you like to be in charge, making decisions?

## CALCULATE YOUR REPUTATION POINTS

*This quiz by Barbara Reinhold appears at content.monster.com.au/management/reputation/.*

In company life, nothing is more important than your reputation. Have you been taking good care of yours? To what extent (Not true, Slightly true, True or Very true) do each of the following statements apply to you?

1. At my last performance review, my manager told me I was doing a really good job.

2. I have made positive connections with people in other departments, so I know what's going on and therefore how to position myself.

3. I often ask for new assignments that stretch me and let me develop new skills.

4. I ask for feedback from my supervisors and colleagues about how my work is going, and I make changes if I need to.

5. I know the things I'm not very good at and I make it a point to overcome those weaknesses.

6. I have worked out who has influence in the organisation and how to get myself noticed in a positive way.

7. I volunteer for community service projects or other organisational efforts that will give me a chance to meet people and make a good impression.

8. I make a point of being cheerful and friendly at work.

9. I'm careful to be seen as a positive person at work and I resist cynical or critical comments.

10. I know what my manager needs from me and I provide it.

## WHAT'S YOUR WORK STYLE?

*This quiz by Barbara Reinhold appears at content.monster.com.au/tools/ quizzes/workstyle/.*

How does your personality affect your work style? Based on psychotherapist Carl Jung's concept of temperaments, we've come up with our own names for four different work styles. Take these questions to find out yours. Each question has a response that reflects each work style. Then, we suggest you take the quiz again, applying it to your boss, co-worker, or mentor, to figure out if you are working together in the best way possible.

Use this quiz to ask yourself: Have you been trying to function in a way that conflicts with how you're really wired? Have you been approaching others in ways that don't match their types?

1. *What's the best way to work on projects?*
- Let's work independently and then check back in a few days. It's important to keep options open for a while to get the best plan.
- Let's make a timetable right away, so we know who's going to do what and when each part is due to be completed.
- I want to think of the long-term implications before jumping into the project—I'd also rather brainstorm with a few people whose ideas I really respect.
- I want to be sure that everyone feels included and has a role they feel good about in finishing the project.

2. *What's important for success?*
- Finish things correctly and on time.
- Be optimistic and upbeat, so that people will want to work together.
- Be effective in a crisis.
- Ask questions to be sure you're on the right track.

3. *What improvements would you like to see at work?*
- We need to give people more chances to develop their talents.
- We have too much talk and too little work.
- We've forgotten what has worked in the past and have too many new ideas on the table.
- We need to analyse the way we're structured.

4.  *What do you need to work effectively?*
- To be able to ask questions and involve lots of people.
- Flexibility and independence.
- Clear expectations.
- The chance to experiment with new ideas.

5.  *What drives you nuts?*
- Doing things the same old way for no good reason.
- Carelessness.
- Insensitive people.
- Too many rules.

6.  *What complaints do you have about yourself?*
- I'm a control freak.
- I don't care enough about people.
- I always fly by the seat of my pants.
- My skin is too thin.

7.  *Who do you like to work with?*
- Flexible, adaptable people.
- Smart, interesting people.
- Enthusiastic, optimistic people.
- Dependable people.

8.  *What situations bug you?*
- When people don't think about what they're saying.
- When people forget the human cost of business decisions.
- When people are too emotional.
- When people are too nit-picky about details.

## ARE YOU READY FOR A JOB CHANGE?

*And now for a more lighthearted one by Peter Newfield. It appears at content.monster.com.au/tools/quizzes/careerchange/.*

Money isn't the only reason to change jobs. Sometimes the work environment, stress, lack of cooperation among staff, and personality conflicts can contribute to unhappiness and dissatisfaction with your job. Answer True or False to the following statements to determine whether you should be considering new opportunities for improved job satisfaction and greater personal, as well as financial, rewards.

- You get that feeling of dread in the pit of your stomach when you hear the 'Tick, Tick, Tick' on '60 Minutes' on Sunday evenings.
- You oversleep in the mornings and/or take longer lunch hours.
- You envy Gilligan's lifestyle when you catch late night reruns of that 1960s sitcom.
- You have to pinch your palm, bite the inside of your lip, or plan weekend errands in your head just to stay awake during staff meetings.
- You still have 'Update resumé' on your 'Things to do' list from last year.
- Your mortgage and credit card bills are giving you nightmares.
- You question your accomplishments after learning at your recent high-school reunion that the lowest achiever in your class drives a brand-new Land Rover and just returned from a Mount Everest climbing expedition.
- You've used up all of the 'dead relative' excuses for taking time off from work.
- You walk around coughing loudly the day before any office social function, so that you can call in sick the next day.
- You count the cleaning lady as one of your closest friends at work.
- Your department has seen so much employee turnover that you are considered to be senior after only two years on the job.
- You are borrowing money on a weekly basis from your ten-year-old child, and he's starting to charge interest.

Just to reiterate, these tests and quizzes on their own will not be life-altering. What they will do is tell you the type of person you really are and make you think about where you want to go in a career, and whether your present position is helping you get there. After all, looking inside is the first step towards change – it's all in the mind.

## CASE STUDY
## From Foreign Currency Trader to Turf Supplier: Adam, 33

By the time he was in his early 20s Adam was living a life some people would consider a dream. He was working in the money market as an international currency trader, with all the money and perks that came with it.

Some ten years later he had walked away from this high-pressure job, handed back his credit cards and unlimited expense account and started driving a delivery truck for a friend. He never looked back and has never been happier. 'There is no comparison with the money I was earning then and what I earn now, but the lifestyle I now have wins out every time,' he said.

Adam started working part-time in the money market, while study-ing at university. After seven years as a foreign currency trader he left to work for a company that supplied online information for media organisations. He then joined a public relations firm that was sold a short time later, leaving Adam without a job.

I vowed then I would never wear a suit to work again. I'd just about had it. A friend who supplied and laid instant turf asked me to drive his truck. I didn't even have a truck licence but I showed up at 5.30 a.m. to do a day's driving and enjoyed it so much I kept doing it for the next twelve months.

At the end of the year Adam told his friend he could build up the business, but he needed equity. They formed an easy-going 50–50 partnership that would have become a lot more complicated with the introduction of the GST.

'It was a very simple arrangement, but the book-keeping needed for the GST would have been a nightmare,' Adam explains. 'We decided to form two businesses. He grows the turf and I buy it from him and lay it.' Adam's small but growing business provides him with a comfortable income, but he says the money is not the major issue.

I wanted a career where I could be my own boss, not answerable to anyone. It is a seasonal job. At Christmas I had nine men working for me. At slow times I might have three or four. If I need to make more money I grab the tools and lay the turf myself. If I want to spend time with my three kids I make sure the crews are all set up and go pick the children up from school or watch them at swimming lessons.

I don't work weekends unless things are frantic. I can take a holiday with the family without any stress. That is worth a lot more than money as far as I am concerned.

That is not to say that Adam does not want to build up his business. He does, but not purely for monetary reasons.

'I want to build it up, but not to sell it,' he says. 'I want the business to grow because I think it is a great opportunity. It just suits me perfectly. It is healthy, outdoor work and I am my own boss. It might not be for everyone, but it is a career which suits me down to the ground.'

Literally, it would seem.

# 4

# someone to lean on

Quite often the crucial question in a working life isn't 'Should I make a career move?' It is 'How do I make a career move?' As we have seen, in many cases the only thing stopping someone from taking decisive action is themself. They need to move, they are ready to move, but they are not emotionally or mentally able to make the move. In simple terms, they need someone to hold their hand. Earlier we suggested putting yourself through a regular personal re-evaluation test. Nothing elaborate, just a simple Q & A. Are you happy? Are you challenged? Are you fulfilled? If the answer to any of these questions is no, the logical step is to put the wheels of change in motion. But for some people, taking that small first step appears as intimidating as leaping across a chasm. They need help. It might be a case of asking a trusted friend or mentor, a family member or workmate who will no doubt give the best advice they can, but often advice is not enough. People who are not comfortable with change or whose personal situation makes change particularly risky need more. They may need the practical help of a professional career-guidance counsellor. They may require the psychological 'permission to be oneself' that we have already outlined. Or it may take a combination of both, in the form of a personal coach.

## PERSONAL COACHING

Personal coaching (also known as 'life-coaching') is a phenomenon that started in the USA around 1990 and has spread rapidly around the world. It is an enormous growth industry worth $100 billion worldwide. The respected magazine *Fortune* described it as the USA's second fastest growing industry, behind information technology.

So what is personal coaching? According to the International Coach Federation (ICF), the world's largest professional association of business and personal coaches with 175 chapters in most States of the USA and 28 countries:

> Coaching is an ongoing relationship between coach and client, which focuses on the client taking action toward the realisation of their visions, goals or desires. Coaching uses a process of inquiry and personal discovery to build the client's level of awareness and responsibility and provides the client with structure, support and feedback. The coaching process helps clients both define and achieve professional and personal goals faster and with more ease than would be possible otherwise.

The ICF currently has some 200 coaches on its books in Australia and expects to have over 1000 by 2003. Clients will pay anything from $300 to $1000 a month for their weekly interactions, designed to help them get more from their lives.

Many people who have used the services of a personal coach liken themselves to athletes. If a world-champion runner, swimmer or football player can raise their performance level by using a coach, they say, why shouldn't they? After all, even the world's highest-paid athlete, Tiger Woods, has a coach. But personal coaching goes further than just performance in one single area. Unlike specialised sports coaching, it covers all aspects of the client's life. A coach can help with relationships (both professional and personal), financial planning and, of course, career guidance.

## HOW A COACH CAN HELP

In 1998 the International Coach Federation polled 210 coaching clients, all of whom had had a formal relationship with an ICF coach, regularly meeting for strategy sessions over an average of nine months. The second most frequently listed function of the coach, the survey found, was in the area of career guidance. Respondents said they turned to their coach for help with:

- time management (80.5%)
- career guidance (74.3%)
- business advice (73.8%)
- advice on relationships/family issues (58.6%)
- physical/wellness issues (51.9%)
- personal issues (45.2%)
- goal-setting (39.5%)
- financial guidance (38.1%)
- creativity (11%).

The survey also found that:
- Almost one quarter of people who confided in a personal coach said it led directly to a change in career.
- 50% of the respondents said they confided in their coach as much as their best friend, spouse or therapist; 12% say they confided in their coach more than in anyone else.
- 84.8% of respondents said the main role of their coach was

as a sounding board – to listen and give honest feedback.
- 78.1% called the coach a motivator, 56.7% a friend, 50.5% a mentor, 46.7% a business consultant and 41% a teacher.

The outcomes that clients most often attributed to their coaching were:
- a higher level of self-awareness (67.6%)
- smarter goal-setting (62.4%)
- a more balanced life (60.5%)
- lower stress levels (57.1%)
- self-discovery (52.9%)
- more self-confidence (52.4%)
- improvement in quality of life (43.3%)
- enhanced communication skills (39.5%)
- project completion (35.7%)
- health or fitness improvement (33.8%)
- better relationship with boss or co-workers (33.3%)
- better family relationships (33.3%)
- increased energy (31.9%)
- more fun (31.9%)
- more income (25.7%)
- stopped a bad habit (25.7%)
- a change in career (24.3%)
- more free time (22.9%).

While coaching was once looked upon as the latest self-improvement fad – the 1990s equivalent of the 1960s 'personal guru' – it has rapidly become recognised as an essential development tool for the individual.

So seriously is the concept of personal coaching taken that the University of Sydney offers a post-graduate course in coaching psychology – the first of its kind in the world. The coaches work closely with the Coaching Psychology Unit that is attached to the university's Psychology Department and headed up by coaching psychologist Tony Grant. Coaching psychology has been described as 'sitting at the intersection of counselling and clinical and organisational psychology'. Coaching is a form of consulting, but the coach stays with the client to help implement the new skills, changes and goals to ensure that they really happen. However, coaches do not try to 'fix' a client; it is entirely up to the client to take the action in order to change their life. As one US coach put it: 'A therapist helps a person get from dysfunctional to functional, a coach helps a person get from functional to exceptional.'

In the USA, business giants IBM, AT&T and Kodak have eagerly embraced coaching. Ernst & Young recently made coaching available for all of its partners. In Australia the trend is less developed, but steadily growing. An ANZ spokesperson, for example, says six to ten of the bank's senior executives have personal coaches and that this type of support has been around for a number of years, either through an external coach or under the auspices of the company's HR department. A recent survey of 34 major Australian companies found that leading firms, such as Hyatt International and Ray White Real Estate, were among those using coaches. More than half the companies surveyed said they provided external personal coaching to help with career development, problem solving and career issues such as promotion. The companies surveyed were from the banking and finance, professional services, resources, telecommunications, food, transport and manufacturing sectors.

Issues that coaches often work on with their clients include:
- business planning, budgeting and goal-setting
- integrating business and personal life for balance
- taking a project to completion
- handling business or personal problems

- making key decisions and designing strategies
- prioritising all actions and projects
- catching up and keeping ahead in business
- training, developing and managing staff
- increasing sales substantially or filling a practice
- turning around a difficult situation.

## WHY THE NEED FOR PERSONAL COACHES?

A recent US report linked the growth of personal coaching directly to changes in the fabric of society both inside and out of the working environment. Reasons included:

- Supervisors in expanding companies are faced with growing responsibilities for which they are not prepared. They find themselves applying traditional solutions to new problems.
- Society's mobility has taken away close family and friends, leaving some people without support systems.
- Due to downsizing, some companies are trying to do more with less, leaving employees stressed and feeling like they've never caught up.
- Downsizing is leading to more people being self-employed, sometimes without much experience in owning and operating a business.

Recently, in an article in the *Australian Financial Review,* John Rose, professor of commerce and business administration at the Melbourne Business School, described personal coaching as a natural extension of the mentoring system used by many large companies in Australia. The growth of personal coaching, he said, reflected a shift away from 'analytical, quantitative business skills' towards more personal, interpersonal and organisational skills. Many business schools, including his own, now offer courses in this field. 'Perhaps we're just seeing a more formal approach than we've seen before,' he said. 'For instance, senior executives have often asked for tuition in areas such as public speaking, written communications or the way in which they present. All of those areas would fall under coaching.' Professor Rose said personal coaching was a natural development from the constant evaluation, including 360-degree feedback, now used to chart the performance of senior executives.

Referring to a coach as a confidante of enormous value is a comment that comes through time and again in the literature about personal coaching and, of course, in our own personal experience through career management services. As we said earlier in our chapter on the psychological aspects of career change, having someone to 'externalise' with is absolutely vital. But having the *right* person to externalise with is even more important.

Personal coaches provide a listening service with no strings attached. The personal coach has no hidden agenda. Their job is to help you become the best you can be. When you speak to your coach, you know you are the most important person in the conversation and any effect of your talk can only be positive. Ellen Schulz, 42, an MBA-qualified business consultant-coach in the US, works with staff at Fortune 500 companies that are in the throes of downsizing. As she told the *Denver Post*: 'There's so much workplace competition. People don't dare share their vulnerability. Your manager may be the same person putting you on the cut list.' Knowing that the person you are talking to brings no personal issues or baggage to the table can often provide just the impetus needed to make the most important move of your life.

## HOW TO COMMUNICATE WITH YOUR COACH

How you actually communicate with that person varies. Some coaches prefer to work by telephone. One coaching team interviewed for a US publication said they believed communicating by phone forced them to focus on what the client was saying rather than on extraneous information like appearances, facial expression or body language that can sometimes get in the way of the message. It also allowed them to help clients across the country. Another coach in the same article was just as adamant that the sessions should be in-person.

> I work one-on-one with a client. The concept is to help the client identify personal needs in terms of leadership or organisational style, articulate those needs and develop a strategy and timeline for resolving or meeting those needs. Coaching is much better done face-to-face than telephonically; only then can I ascertain directly what the client is doing.
>
> People seeking coaching have come to the sudden realisation that there is something more to life – some know what it is, but they usually don't. Coaching is for anybody who wants more in life and is willing to take action to accomplish their goal.

Asked what aspect of their lives clients most wanted to work on, the coach responded: 'There isn't a most. Everybody comes to coaching from a different place. A common thread is that our clients want something different in their lives and see coaching as a vehicle for getting it.'

For further information about personal coaching or to find a coach:
- www.coachfederation.org
- www.coachuoz.com.au

## CASE STUDIES
### Personal Coaching Clients' Stories

Befitting a phenomenon that has grown so quickly in such a short space of time, personal coaching has received blanket media coverage around the world. Feature stories relate numerous case studies of people who have received the personal support needed to kick-start the process of career change. Some of those featured in Australian and US publications such as *The Age*, *The Courier-Mail*, *Australian Financial Review*, *Las Vegas Sun* and *Denver Post* follow.

- **Pauline**, 41, who believes coaching has helped her navigate the challenges of both her professional and personal life. 'When you are a mother of two, with a husband who works overseas a lot and are running a business, it all gets very stressful and you have a lot of clutter in your life,' said Pauline, who is also in personal development consultancy. 'A life coach helps you to get rid of the clutter and see life in a more balanced way.'
- **Penny**, 32, employed a life coach to help her establish the lifestyle she had always dreamt about and a career that would satisfy her desire to help others.

> I was a bit scattered and all over the place with what I wanted to do. I had been working for the past couple of years just getting some cash coming in. My mum had been really sick and I nursed her until her death, which meant my husband and I had spent two years not really living our own lives. I discovered it wasn't so much about creating a career, as it was creating a lifestyle. My husband was unhappy in his career and so we decided to launch our own house-renovating business. I never dreamt that renovating houses would be a job that would bring an income sufficient to allow us to create the lifestyle we had

always wanted. The hardest thing was taking a chance. I had
to trust that the ideas we were planning could work. Marc,
my coach, really helped me push my safety zone. The result
is that it has created exactly the flexible lifestyle we want.

- **Michael**, 37, an executive manager, saw life coaching as a way to
safeguard the future of his marriage and family life.

> When we got married we had a picture of how we
> wanted our marriage to be – and it wasn't. Both of us
> work full-time. We get home at 7 p.m. most nights and,
> after having dinner and putting our sons to bed, we're
> pretty shattered. Twelve months ago, my kids would have
> described me as the grumpy guy they saw on Saturdays.
> If you are driving along the road at 10 km/h and you
> start veering off the edge, you've got plenty of time
> to recover, but when you are going down the road at
> 120 km/h you only need to be one degree off and
> within seconds, you are miles off course.

After completing a workshop and several months of life coaching, Michael said his relationship with his wife and two young sons
was transformed, and his work performance and personal finances
improved. 'Coaching has realigned all aspects of my life. My wife
and I have cleaned up our communication. I now take time to listen and relate to my sons. I've got far better clarity.'

- **Daniel** used to be an accountant for a Sydney car dealership.
At 41, he had got over the notion of having a job for life. Suddenly
he wanted a change. Three years ago he went to a motivational
seminar on career upheaval in the USA. He took the advice of
a coach, relocated to Melbourne to study, and followed his dream
into the music business as an audio technician.

- **Lisa** was unhappy with the career choice she made when she swapped one middle-management position in the employment industry for another, supposedly similar one, in a large public sector organisation. While her professional duties hadn't altered dramatically, her work environment and the company culture had. 'Changing positions was a hasty decision and I'm paying the price.' Rather than repeat her mistakes, she is biding her time in her current job with the help of her recently appointed life coach.

> When you apply for a job, quite often you base it around the role itself and the skills you bring to it, without bringing into it the culture of the work environment and how it will interfere with your outside working life. My coach and I are identifying what I feel I really need to be happy with my working environment. I was doing twelve-hour days, which was too much for me. I'm hoping that the life coach will help me find a balance between work and family.

It costs Lisa about $550 a month, but she believes it is money well spent. For her outlay she receives six personalised sessions: four half-hour telephone conversations (most coaches only operate this way and never meet their clients), and two one-and-a-half-hour face-to-face meetings.

Lisa's life coach, a former psychologist, believes good listening skills are one of the most important attributes for effective life coaching. There is, he says, a clear distinction between the roles of life coach and psychologist. 'One of the ways in which coaching is really different from therapy is that we look at the question "How can I be what I want to be?" Whereas therapy is looking at "Why am I the way I am?" One is really introspective and one is really action-oriented,' he said.

One of the first tasks Lisa's coach set for her was to ask

questions of her former colleagues in order to discover and recognise the way others see her. She discussed the results of her exploration with her coach at their next meeting. 'We're about guiding clients to take initiative,' he said. 'Lisa would also like to write children's books, so one of the first things I told her to do was to re-read her childhood favourite, *The Narnia Chronicles* by C.S. Lewis.' He also told her to make contact with authors she respects, to ask how they started their careers.

- **Mike** is a lawyer whose business was thriving, but who wanted more out of life.

> My law firm was going very well, and I was busy but I wanted to grow and I wanted to increase everything, like have more time for my family. My coach and I crystallised where I was at. At the time I met him I was by myself in a serviced office, and we sat down and planned exactly what my ideal office would look like – and the way I wanted to expand. The whole experience has already helped me. The best thing about the life coach is that the information I get will always be objective. It's not about the coach, it's all about the player.

- **Robin**, a scriptwriter, believes coaching has dramatically influenced his career, relationships and general health. His first film script is with a US agent, with another in the pipeline. 'My life has changed completely in the last 15 months,' he said. 'I'm now in control of my life. I can't control outside events, but I'm master of my own destiny.' Apart from introducing a sense of discipline into his working life (deadlines are no longer the terror they once were), Robin, said coaching had given him the strength to address deep-seated health and emotional issues. He said having a personal coach filled a requirement that even the closest male confidant could never hope to meet.

# 5

# the search begins

The first step towards a new career is to find the direction in which you should head, then comes the task of narrowing it down to one job. In considering a new direction, you must be open to change. Perhaps you are totally unsuited to the area in which you presently work. Perhaps your compass only needs a slight adjustment. Either way, be creative.

Often the best fit for a person is a job that they didn't even know existed. A good starting point is to look at the employment advertisements in the newspaper and on the Internet for several weeks. You will see a pattern emerging as you circle the ads that are of interest to you. And, you never know, you could see something that seems perfect for you – something that, up until you saw that advert, you had never even considered.

## MATCHING THE PERSONAL AND THE PROFESSIONAL

What will spark your interest? Nine times out of ten, it will be the connection between the job and the person you are when you are away from work. It is a fact that most successful people are able to just be themselves when they are at work. There is no 'work face' and 'home face'; there is no need for a mask. There is just the one persona: that of a person being themselves and enjoying what they do. Therefore, the perfect fit for you is a job that allows you to be yourself and express yourself through your work. Easier said than done? Sometimes, but it is certainly not impossible.

In many instances, it is not a case of someone not being able to achieve their dream career, it is a case of them not knowing what their dream career is. Once you have found a different path, it is imperative that you get on to that path. Trouble is, the path you are on, and the path you want to get on to do not always intersect. Or if there is a crossroad, it tends not to be a clearly marked intersection with traffic lights and a crossing guard. You might have to clear away some undergrowth first; you might even have to go backwards before you go forward, but eventually you will make it if you want to badly enough.

Sometimes it will require learning a whole new set of skills but, generally speaking, if the fit is right, the basic skills will be right. For instance, a bank manager might want to fulfil a lifelong ambition to become a croupier in a casino. His friends might think he is crazy, but actually the basic requirements of the two jobs are very similar. A bank manager must have an eye for detail, must be numerate, patient and enjoy dealing with people. So must a croupier. It is not a common career change, but it is definitely a possible one. Similarly, for the scientist who wishes to become a science teacher, or the technical expert who has a long-held desire to enter the sales department of a company that deals in his area of expertise – if the desire exists and the people skills are there, the knowledge is certainly already there. It is just a case of putting the two together and then finding the industry, or better still, the organisation, to aim for.

## CHOOSING FOR THE FUTURE

In order to choose a new area in which to move, you have to be something of a fortune-teller. Not only should you head in a direction that suits your skills and interests, you also have to peer into the future, and take a punt on what you think is going to grow with you, and also is an area that is going to thrive and survive into the future.

You know what your heart tells you. There are certain career paths that will always appeal to you because of life-long interests and passions. What you have to do is marry those interests with a position in an industry that can take you where you want to go. At this point, what your heart tells you must take a back seat to what your head tells you. Even then, a good deal of luck will be needed.

Choosing an industry or market sector that is going to grow is similar to speculating on the stock market. Unfortunately, as any market analyst will tell you, trying to predict the future is not an exact science. It wasn't too long ago that dot com industries were being hailed as the new frontier. Today there are many unhappy investors (and retrenched dot com workers) who will attest to the fact that any boom, no matter how spectacular, can be short-lived. This experience should serve as a cautionary tale for anyone looking to change a career path hastily or for the wrong reasons.

Investing in your future is little different to investing on the market. Some investors go for a high return and therefore must be prepared for a high-risk investment. Others will go for the long-term and put their money into blue chip stocks that, while offering lower returns, are a lower risk. The same applies to a change of employment direction.

## CHECKING YOUR PRIORITIES, DESIRES AND NEEDS

The first step in choosing the new direction is to give yourself a strict self-appraisal. What sort of person are you, and what are you looking for? What are your financial and emotional constraints? If you are single, with no commitments and money in the bank, obviously your priorities will be different to those of a married person with children and a large mortgage. For your career to work for you, it must fulfil not only your desires, but also your needs. Only you can say what your dream career is, and to do so with conviction you must be 100 per cent honest with yourself. So ask yourself the questions.

What do you want and what can you afford to risk?

If the answer is that you are looking for thrills, spills and a fast buck, you will find it in a high-risk business, which, by its very nature, is prepared to offer higher salaries. You will find these organisations involved in technology, new products, or more cyclical industries in sectors susceptible to the vagaries of the economy. On the other hand, if you are looking for stability, high job security and an opportunity to work steadily through to the top in an established firm, you will find it in any number of industries or government agencies. The key is to find the best fit: the position and firm that most suits your desires, needs and personality. Having found that industry, the first step is to get your foot in the door.

## GETTING YOUR FOOT IN THE DOOR

There are several ways to do this:
- directly approach the prospective employer by letter, email, telephone or through their web site
- approach a recruitment company and ask them to place you in a suitable organisation in the sector you are seeking
- network with contacts already involved in the industry or related ones
- answer advertisements (using both print media and Internet as your sources).

The Internet plays a major role in the employment industry and is only going to grow. The speed with which the Internet is revolutionising the art of finding the right job – or the right person for a job – is staggering. It has made a change of career both easier and faster, so that nowadays the first move in any career change should be to turn on your computer, whether it is to find out more about prospective employers or to lodge your resumé.

When it comes to finding new jobs or new employees, the Internet is a monster – happily, a friendly monster. For where once you needed to 'go out' and find a job, thanks to the Internet, the job can now find you! If you know the name of a company that you feel would suit your employment needs, you should go straight to their web site. This will not only give you more of a feel for the company and what they do, but in some cases, tell you immediately what opportunities are available. Microsoft, for example, lists all of its available jobs on its web site. It estimates that 50 per cent of jobs in the organisation are filled in this manner.

> The Internet has made it possible for work to find people, rather than just the other way round.

It is obvious that the majority of progressive organisations will follow Microsoft's lead over the next few years, but that will complement online career portals, as they will represent the total market. In effect, these sites (both corporate and portals) have eliminated the need to write speculative letters to companies in the hope of being offered an interview. Thanks to the Internet, you need only lodge your resumé in cyberspace in order to have access to thousands of prospective employers worldwide. The vast majority of these resumés are lodged anonymously. You give your qualifications, but not your name. An employer will lodge their requirements on the web, the computer will make a match, and you will be on your way.

While it might sound like something from the realm of science fiction, the fact is that Internet employment is the way of the present as much as of the future. It is estimated that by the year 2005, there will be 100 million resumés in cyberspace. The attraction is obvious. For the employee seeking to make a change, there are the benefits of reach and anonymity. The Internet doesn't make a selection, just a connection. The prospective employer will see the resumé and ask for more details. It might be many steps down the track before you have to give your name.

The connection might be with an employer or organisation that you never considered approaching. It might even be a company that didn't know it was looking for someone like you – until your resumé came to their attention. From the employer's point of view it comes down to this. There are two ways to attract and screen 1000 resumés: they can have the postie drop off bags of mail at their office and start the task of going through them; or they can push a button and let the computer do more of the initial work.

It is best to register your resumé on a good general site, as well as specific sites catering for specialised fields and industries. Once you

Employment web sites are available all over the world and include:
- for jobs in Australia: Monster.com.au, seek.com.au and mycareer.com.au
- for jobs in the UK: stepstone.com
- for jobs in Asia and the Pacific rim: Monster.com
- for jobs in the USA: flipdog.com and hotjobs.com.

have narrowed your search down to a specific industry or, better still, a small number of companies, you should begin your research. Again, go straight to the company web site. If the annual report isn't already on the site, track it down, either through the stock exchange or by contacting the company and asking for a copy. They will send one to you or advise where you can view it. Look for any recent media articles about the company. These may also be available on the Internet or through news organisations, for a small fee.

Unofficial sources are a good fount of information. Network informally: talking to employees or former employees is invaluable. When you reach the interview stage, a good recruiter will be able to give a wealth of anecdotal information. Any information you glean from any or all of these sources should be added to the mix and, if approached with an open mind, will influence you to make the right decision.

## IS IT A PERFECT MATCH?

Instinct is a strong element in deciding whether or not to join an organisation. It is surprising how often one will instinctively make the right decision. Again, this comes down to 'fit'. You will instinctively know if you will be comfortable in a certain work environment. If this feeling does not come easily, chances are you and the organisation will never be right for each other.

How do you know whether you will be comfortable? Well, should you go through the interview process and actually be interviewed by company executives, take close note. They are representative of the people with whom you will be working. If you like them, and the way they conduct themselves, chances are you will like the company where they work. But don't be afraid to conduct your own interview. Remember, you are looking them over just as much as they are looking you over. Ask questions about the culture of the company: 'What sort of people work here? Could you describe the most successful people here?' All this information will help you to decide whether you are likely to fit in.

A key question is: 'What is the percentage of staff turnover?' If it is over 20 or 25 per cent (a relatively high proportion) you can assume one of three things: there are cultural issues, the company is in a volatile sector, or it is going through a change in direction and business mix, and hence needs new and different skills. The follow-up question is 'Why do they leave?' Take note of the answer, but it is not unreasonable to make your own assumptions. The fact is that companies are made up of people and the majority of people tend to leave a company not because they do not like the work, but for other reasons.

As well as a consistently high staff turnover rate, there are a number of telltale warning signs. To begin with, take heed of the press stories relating to the company. Are they balanced stories written by a reputable journalist, or unsourced positive puff pieces. If the latter, they are usually the result of company-generated public relations or paid advertorial rather than journalistic research.

Secondly, be wary if a position is offered to you too quickly. If after one interview you are told you have the job, step back and reconsider. One quick chat is not enough on which to base a major life change. The people who interviewed you do not know you any more than you know them. As a rule of thumb, the more involved the employment process, the better. Ideally, you will have had assessment tests, at least two interviews – the lot. You want the company to be as sure about you as you are about them. This should not be a simple process on either side. The company employing you should not take its decision any more lightly than you will take yours. After all, while to the employer you might be seen as an answer to an immediate need, to you this job is part of a journey. It may be the final destination, or just a stop along the way. Either way, it is part of your dream, and you must be sure this is a step in the right direction.

## CASE STUDY
## From Teacher to Sports Administrator:
## Mark, 47

When Mark finished high school with good marks but no real idea of what he wanted to do for the rest of his life, he enrolled at university and studied Commerce. Three years later he graduated with his degree, but was still unsure of what direction he should take.

Mark returned to his hometown, thought he might try teaching and 'just on spec' decided to contact some local schools. The first couldn't help him, the second hired him, so, for the next 23 years, Mark was a teacher.

At first he found teaching challenging and stimulating. While teaching at the school, he gained his Diploma of Education and later taught at an international school in Papua New Guinea for three years. He then returned to a country high school in Australia.

But little by little the challenge of teaching was replaced by a feeling of drudgery and, without admitting it to himself, he wanted a change.

It was a combination of factors. I felt I was getting stale and found myself moving further and further away from the interests of my students. Instead of working in an environment where I felt I was sharing something with my students and we were both benefiting from the interaction, the classroom had become a battlefield.

There were also problems associated with the distance he had to commute: one of the major reasons for people becoming dissatisfied with their jobs. For twelve years Mark worked at a school that required making a 160-kilometre round trip each day.

'I began to resent time pressures which were running every aspect of my life,' Mark said. 'But I suppose in effect it all boiled down to this: the initial challenges in teaching were no longer as stimulating as they had once been.'

As a parent of three children (aged 20, 17 and 10) Mark had been involved in their sporting interests, as well as his own. It was this link to sport that would lead Mark on to a new career path. As well as watching two of his children play in a particular sport, Mark had worked as a volunteer, helping arrange fixtures and officiating on event days. On one occasion, while on long-service leave, Mark had worked full-time for the sporting body during a week-long tournament.

It was this regular volunteer work, his enthusiasm and the methodical, well-organised manner in which he had carried out his tasks that led to an 'out of the blue' offer. Mark was approached by the executive director of the sport and asked if he would consider a full-time management position.

For Mark, while the offer was unexpected and eventually life-changing, it gave him the chance to alter the direction of his career and, at the same time, to use organisational and people skills honed through years in the teaching environment. After careful consideration, he accepted the offer.

I had always had an interest in sport – although, apart from the fact that two of my children played the game, not specifically in the sport in which I now found myself working. But importantly, this job brought me back in touch with my community – something that had been lost because of the hours I spent commuting. Even more, it allowed me to con-nect more with my family, especially my youngest child who had only known me as 'the commuter'.

The change of job obviously made an immediate impact on Mark's working life, but, more importantly, on his lifestyle. Three years after making the change from teacher to sports administrator, the benefits were obvious to Mark – if not to all his former colleagues.

> I certainly feel more in control and less ruled by the clock. Although the working hours are sometimes longer, there is greater flexibility in my day and general working life. My family is very supportive of the move, but my old teaching mates will often ask 'Is everything all right?' in a tone which really seems to be saying, 'When are you coming back to teaching?'

The answer is, not in the foreseeable future. Mark is very happy where he is right now, although, after experiencing one change in direction, he cannot say for certain that it will be the last.

'Have I found my dream career?' he asks. 'I don't know whether one exists – but in the meantime, I'm very happy to get stuck into my work every day, and that is not something I could have said three and a half years ago.'

# 6

# tools for opening the door

Once you have decided where you want to go, the next step is to get face to face with someone who will help you get there. A recruitment specialist can make the next few steps along your career path a lot less rocky, pointing the way and maybe even holding your hand when you appear to be wandering off track. But whether you have a guide or not, the fact remains that at some stage it will all be up to you. Your advisers cannot sit with you in the interview room or help you break the ice in a new work environment. That is your job. And regardless of who is advising you, there are a number of steps you must take before you even get to base camp. These are writing a resumé and arranging an interview.

Being granted an interview with a prospective employer can be relatively easy if it has been arranged by a consultant or you have answered an advertisement. But what if there is no ad in the 'Positions Vacant' section of the newspaper? What if there is no job on offer? That is where two things will determine whether you make the breakthrough you have dreamt about: your determination, and your ability to use a telephone.

## THE TELEPHONE

Yes, that's right. In this computer age, with IT opening up more and more advanced methods of interviewing, it is often your skill with the humble telephone that will determine whether you even get to the starting line. In an excerpt drawn from J. Michael Farr's 1995 book *Getting the Job You Really Want* (and reprinted on Monster.com), the author suggests that preparing a phone 'script' that enables you to get an interview is as important as what you say when you are facing the interviewers. Farr offers the following tips.

### Get to the hiring authority

You need to get directly to the person who would supervise you. Unless you want to work in the personnel department, you wouldn't normally ask to talk to someone who does. Depending on the type and size of the organisation you are calling, you should have a pretty good idea of the title of the person who would supervise you. In a small business you might ask to speak to the 'person in charge'. In a larger one, you would ask for the name of the person who is in charge of a particular department.

### Get the name of a person

If you don't have the name of the person you need to speak to, ask for it. For example, ask for the name of the person in charge of the accounting department if that is where you want to work. Usually, you will be given the supervisor's name and your call will be transferred to him or her immediately. When you do get a name, get the correct spelling and write it down right away. Then you can use that person's name in your conversation.

### Get past the receptionist

In some cases, receptionists and secretaries will try to screen out your call. If they find out you are looking for a job, they may transfer you to the personnel department or ask you to send an application or resumé. Here are some things you can do to keep from getting screened out:

- Call back a day later and say you are getting ready to send some correspondence to the person who manages such and such. You want to use the correct name and title, so request this information. This is true since you will be sending them something soon. And this approach usually gets you what you need. Thank them and call back in a day or so. Then ask for the supervisor or manager by name.

- Call when the secretary is out to lunch and you may get right through. Other good times are just before and after normal work hours. Less experienced staff members are likely to answer the phones and put you right through. The boss also might be in early or working late.

**When referred by someone else**

It is always best to be referred by someone else. If this is the case, immediately give the name of the person who suggested you call. For example, say: 'Hello, Ms Beetle. Joan Bugsby suggested I give you a call.' If the receptionist asks why you are calling, say: 'A friend of Ms Beetle's suggested I give her a call about a personal matter.' When a friend of the employer recommends that you call, you usually get right through.

**When calling someone you know**

Sometimes using your telephone script will not make sense. For example, if you are calling someone you know, you would normally begin with some friendly conversation before getting to the purpose of your call. Then, you could use your phone script by saying something like: 'The reason I called is to let you know

I am looking for a job, and I thought you might be able to help. Let me tell you a few things about myself. I am looking for a position as . . .' Then continue with the rest of your phone script here. There are many other situations where you will need to adapt your basic script. Use your judgment on this. With practice, it becomes easier.

The primary goal of a phone contact is to get an interview. To succeed, you must be ready to get past the first and even the second rejection. You must practise asking three times for the interview. Here is an example:

*You*: When may I come in for an interview?
*Employer*: I don't have any positions open now . . .
*You*: That's OK, I'd still like to come in to talk to you
about the possibility of future openings.
*Employer*: I really don't plan on hiring within the next
six months or so.
*You*: Then I'd like to come in and learn more about
what you do. I'm sure you know a lot about the industry,
and I am looking for ideas on getting into it and
moving up.

Although this approach does not always work, asking the third time works more often than most people would believe. It is important to learn how to do this, since overcoming initial rejection is a very important part of getting to 'Yes'.

### Arrange a time
If the person agrees to an interview, arrange for a specific date and time. If you are not sure of the correct name or address, call back later and ask the receptionist.

## Sometimes an interview does not make sense

Sometimes you will decide not to ask for an interview. The person may not seem helpful or you may have caught him or her at a busy time. If so, you can take another approach:

- Get a referral by asking for the names of other people who might be able to help you. Find out how to contact them. Then add these new contacts to your job search network.
- If your contact is busy when you call, ask if you can call back. Get a specific time and day to do this, and add the call to your 'To do' list for that day. If you do call back, the employer will be impressed, and may give you an interview for that reason alone.
- Ask to call back from time to time. Ask if you can keep in touch. Maybe the employer will hear of an opening or have some other information for you. Many job seekers get their best leads from a person they have checked back with several times.

## Follow up

It is important to follow up with each person you contact in your search for a job. This includes following up with people in your network, including those you phone. This effort can make a big difference in their remembering and helping you. The best way to follow up is to send a thank-you note to the person who helped you. Send a thank-you note right after the phone call. If you arranged for an interview, send a note saying you look forward to your meeting. If the contact gave you a referral to someone else, send another note telling them how things turned out. Or send a thank-you note telling them you followed up on their suggestion.

Sometimes the direct approach over the telephone will work on its own. Sometimes it is best to send a resumé and cover letter in advance and then follow up with a phone call. The opening line 'I sent you my resumé last week and wondered what you thought of my background' is a good way to start the ball rolling. Either way, at some stage you will have to present your resumé and it is imperative to send a cover letter.

## THE COVER LETTER

So, what is a cover letter? Basically, it should achieve everything you hope to achieve with a cold call over the telephone. According to author L. Michelle Tullier (who is quoted on Monster. com), a cover letter is an introduction, a sales pitch and a proposal for further action all in one. It gives the reader a taste of what is to come, she says, not by simply summarising the resumé, but by highlighting the aspects of your background that will be most relevant to the reader. A cover letter also demonstrates that you can organise your thoughts, express yourself clearly and appropriately – in other words, the cover letter reflects your communication skills and, to some extent, your personality.

Cover letters are typically one-page documents. Like lots of things in life, they have:

- a beginning – usually an introduction saying who you are and why you're writing
- a middle – the sales pitch stating what you have to offer
- an end – the closing in which you propose steps for further action.

These three components often amount to three or four paragraphs, but there are no hard and fast rules about exactly how you should break up the information.

Tullier suggests that if you find yourself struck by writer's block at about the 'Dear Mr or Ms So-and-So' point, then you probably need to take a step back and put some more thought into your cover letter before diving into it. She says asking yourself the following five questions will help you build a foundation for your letter and make the actual writing go much more smoothly.

1.  *What does the prospective employer need?* Which skills, knowledge and experience would be an asset in the job you are targeting?
2.  *What are your objectives?* Are you applying for a specific job, trying to get an interview or simply hoping to get someone to spend ten or fifteen minutes on the phone with you discussing opportunities in general at that organisation?
3.  *What are three to five qualities that you would bring to this employer or this job?* If you are responding to a job listing or classified advertisement, then those qualities should obviously be the job requirements mentioned in the ad. If you are not applying for a specific job opening, then think about which skills, knowledge and experience would typically be valued.
4.  *How can you match your experience to the job?* What are at least two specific accomplishments you can mention that give credence to the qualities you identified in number 3 above?
5.  *Why do you want to work for this particular organisation or person?* What do you know about them? What is it about their products or services, philosophy, mission, organisational culture, goals and needs that relates to your own background, values and objectives?

When you've addressed these five issues, you're ready to go to the keyboard and start hammering out that letter. Tullier suggests the cover letter should be broken down into four main areas:

- the opening
- the sales pitch
- the flattery
- the request for further action.

## The opening

This is where you tell the employer who you are, why you are writing and how you heard about the organisation or the specific opening. The 'who you are' part is a brief introduction, for example, 'I am a final year student at XYZ University graduating in May with a degree in Biology.' Mention only the basic facts about you and your situation, choosing the ones that will be most relevant to the employer. The 'why you're writing' part is where you mention which position you are applying for, or what your job objective is if no specific opening has been advertised. Be sure to say how you heard about the organisation or the job. You might say, for example, 'I saw your listing for a textile designer at the Career Development Office of the University of Technology Sydney' or 'I read about the expansion of your Queensland operations in *The Australian* and am interested in discussing entry-level opportunities that you might have available'.

### The sales pitch

In this section, it's best to get right to the point. The objective of this part of the letter is to list, either in paragraph form or as an actual list of bullet points, the reasons why the reader should see you as a viable candidate. It's best to start with a statement that provides an overview of your qualifications, then go into them more specifically using the examples you identified before you started writing. A typical opening statement might be something like: 'As a graduate in journalism and former intern at *The Sydney Morning Herald*, I offer the following skills and accomplishments.'

### The flattery

And then comes the flattery. This is the 'why them' section of your letter. This is where you flatter the reader a bit by commenting on something positive about the organisation, letting them know why you would want to work there. You might mention the organisation's reputation, sales record, size, corporate culture, management

## The Ten Cardinal Rules of Cover Letter Writing

In *Cover Notes* (published as part of 'The Princeton Review Job Notes Series' in 1997), L. Michelle Tullier lists her cardinal rules of cover letter writing.

1. Tailor your letter as much possible to the target reader and industry.
2. Talk more about what you can do for the prospective employer than about what they can do for you.
3. Convey focussed career goals. Even if you'd be willing to take any job they'd offer you, don't say so.
4. Don't say anything negative about your employment situation or your life in general.
5. Cut to the chase; don't ramble.
6. Don't make empty claims that aren't backed up by examples.
7. Don't write more than one page, unless the prospective employer has asked for a detailed or extended cover letter.
8. Check, recheck and triple check your letter for typos and other errors.
9. Get other people's opinions of your letter before you send it.
10. Keep easily accessible copies of all letters you mail, fax or e-mail, along with a log of when letters were sent, so that you can follow up on them.

philosophy or anything else that they take pride in. Prospective employers like to know that you have chosen them for a reason and that they're not just one of hundreds of companies you're writing to as part of a mass mailing. (Even if you are doing a mass mailing, you must tailor each letter to 'flatter' the reader and show that you've done some research into that organisation or that person.)

### The request for further action

Finally comes the request for further action. Some people think of the final section of a cover letter simply as the closing – but it's much more than that. The closing paragraph isn't just about thanking the reader for taking the time to read your letter or for considering you as a candidate for a job. It's also about where to go from here, about opening the door to further contact. It's where you suggest how to proceed, usually by saying that you will call or e-mail the reader to follow up and see if a meeting can be arranged. The important thing is to end the letter in an assertive, but courteous, way by taking the initiative to follow up.

Once you've got these four sections of the letter completed in terms of content, go back and smooth out any rough edges in your writing and be sure to check for typos, misspellings and grammatical errors. Then you're ready for 'Sincerely' or 'Best Regards' and your signature. Now you're off and running on the road to a great job.

## THE RESUMÉ

All of which brings us to the next step towards getting inside that door: the resumé. There are two main types of resumé:

- The traditional resumé is a chronological listing of your employment history 'topped and tailed' with some relevant information, such as a listing of educational qualifications and interests and hobbies that relate directly to the job for which you are applying.

- The functional resumé, which is suited for those who have a longer employment history and who are perhaps aiming for jobs outside the sphere of their previous employment, gives an outline of skills, rather than an employment history. The functional resumé should start with a brief objective, outlining in one paragraph the position the job seeker hopes to achieve. It should then give a personal profile and a skills summary. The professional experience section should not list employers' names and dates of service, but rather a description and outcome of projects undertaken.

Regardless of which type you choose to use, the resumé is both a selling tool and a list of accomplishments. Yes, it should say what you have done in the past, but it must also say what you are capable of doing in the future. It should be complete, yet concise. And most of all, it should say what you have achieved, not just what positions you have held.

And rest assured of this one cruel fact: if your resumé does not strike a chord with the first link in the chain of command, you will never get that job. Which is probably why many people feel intimidated by the thought of preparing a resumé. The question most often asked by job seekers sitting down to write their resumé is: How long should my resumé be? How can I fit all of my experience onto one page? What can I eliminate and what should be highlighted?

Not long ago job seekers followed the golden rule that no resumé should exceed one page. However, today's job seekers are finding that rule no longer applies. Furthermore, there is conflicting advice from books, counsellors, hiring managers, well-meaning friends and family members.

In this time of mass confusion, the solution is simple: Use common sense. If you are just graduating, have less than five years of work experience or are contemplating a complete career change, a one-page resumé will probably suffice. Some technical and executive job seekers require multiple-page resumés. If you have more than five years of experience and a track record of accomplishments, you will need at least two pages to tell your story.

Remember that your resumé is not an autobiography. Employers are inundated with resumé submissions and are faced with the daunting task of weeding out the good from the bad. The first step involves quickly skimming through resumés and eliminating candidates who clearly are not qualified. Therefore, your resumé needs to pass the skim test.

## The Resumé Skim Test

Does your resumé pass the skim test? To find out, dust off your resumé and ask yourself:

- Can a hiring manager see my main credentials within ten to fifteen seconds?
- Does critical information jump off the page, grabbing the reader's attention?
- Do I effectively sell myself on the top quarter of the first page?

Because resumés are quickly skimmed during the first cull, it is crucial yours gets right to work selling your credentials. Your key selling points need to be prominently displayed at the top of the first page. If an MBA degree is important in your career field, your education shouldn't be buried at the end of a four-page resumé.

An effective way to showcase your key qualifications is to include a 'Career Summary' statement at the top of the first page. The remainder of the resumé should back up the statements made in your summary.

You must be your own editor. Many workers are proud of their careers and feel the information on a resumé should reflect all they've accomplished. However, this document shouldn't contain every detail of your career. It should only include the information that will help you land an interview. Just because something is eliminated from your resumé doesn't mean it never happened; it just means the experience is not useful to your resumé's message. The editing step will be difficult if you are holding on to your past for emotional reasons. If this is the case, show your resumé to a colleague or a professional resumé writer for an objective opinion.

## The Pack-a-Punch Resumé

Here are eight tips to ensure your resumé packs a punch and gets the crucial information across to the reader.

1. **Avoid repeating information.** Did you perform the same or similar job tasks for more than one employer? Instead of repeating job duties, focus on your accomplishments in each position.

2. **Eliminate old experience.** Employers are most interested in what you did recently. If you have a long career history, focus on the last ten to fifteen years. If your early career is important to your current goal, briefly mention the experience without going into the details. For example: Early Career: ABC Company, City, State. Served as Assistant Store Manager and Clerk, 1980–1985.

3. **Don't include irrelevant information.** Avoid listing hobbies and personal information, such as date of birth or marital status. Also, eliminate outdated technical or business skills.

4. **Cut down on job duties.** Many job seekers can trim the fat off their resumés simply by removing long descriptions of job duties or responsibilities. Instead, create a paragraph that briefly highlights the scope of your responsibility and then provide a bulleted list of your most impressive accomplishments.

5. **Remove 'References available upon request'.** Many job seekers waste the valuable last line of the resumé on an obvious statement. Unless you're using this as a design element, remove it.

6. **Use a telegraphic writing style.** Eliminate personal pronouns (I, me, my) and minimise the use of articles (a, an, the) when preparing your resumé.

7. **Edit unnecessary words.** Review your resumé for unnecessary phrases such as 'responsible for' or 'duties include'. The reader understands you were responsible for the tasks listed on your resumé.

8. **Customise your resumé for your job target.** Only include information relevant to your goal. This is particularly important for career changers who need to focus on transferable skills and play down unrelated career accomplishments.

## How to Jazz Up Your Resumé

Here are nine ways to jazz up your experience section to capture the attention of hiring managers.

1. **Ditch the job description.** One of the most common mistakes is to write experience sections that read like job descriptions. The result is a boring recap of job duties with no indication of actual job performance.

2. **Prove your value.** Hiring managers scan your resumé looking for clues about what type of worker you are. If you show that you consistently produced positive results for previous employers, you will be seen as a desirable candidate. The key is to emphasise your accomplishments and provide proof of your potential value.

3. **Quantify results.** Which statement has more impact?

   A. Significantly increased revenues and grew client base between 1997 and 2000.

**B.** Increased revenues from $250 000 in 1997 to $1.5 million in 2000 and tripled client base from 2500 to 7000.

In both cases, the job seeker is trying to convey that they increased revenues and expanded the client base, but statement B measures how well this growth was achieved. Wherever possible, include measurable results of your work. Obviously not everyone can release company performance figures. If presenting this information is a breach of confidentiality, find another way to present your accomplishments. For example, use percentages rather than actual dollar figures.

4. ***Are you up to PAR?*** PAR stands for 'Problem Action Results', and is a good starting point for thinking about your accomplishments. What types of challenges did you face? What actions did you take to overcome the problems? What was the result of your efforts, and how did your performance benefit the company? Write down a list of your PAR accomplishments and incorporate the most impressive into your resumé.

5. ***Lead with your work's outcomes***. An effective strategy is to write the result of your work before listing the problem and action. This allows you to lead with the most compelling aspect of your accomplishment. For example: Reversed an annual $2 million decline in market share by streamlining the benchmark process and building a top-flight sales team.

6. ***Make it readable***. Some resumés use dots or bullets to outline work histories, but this tends to blur duties and accomplishments, which dilutes the impact of achievements. Other resumés use a narrative style to describe work history, which tends to be cumbersome to read, especially for hiring managers who are quickly scanning resumés to extract key information. Instead, use a combination of paragraphs and bullets. For each employer,

provide a brief paragraph that details the scope of your responsibilities. Then create a bulleted list of your top contributions. The bullets draw attention to your accomplishments, while giving the eye a place to rest. Preface accomplishments with headings such as 'Key Accomplishments' or 'Significant Contributions'.

7. **Target your experience to your goal**. Resumés are marketing tools. Your employment history should effectively market you for your current job objective. Focus on accomplishments that relate to your goal and remove job duties and accomplishments that don't support your objective.

8. **Use power words**. The quality of the writing makes or breaks your chances for an interview, so select your words carefully. Avoid dull or stale phrases such as 'responsible for' and 'duties include'.

9. **Be honest.** Studies indicate that job seekers often lie about their work experiences on their resumés. The fact is that with honest and well-written employment histories, even job seekers with less-than-perfect backgrounds will secure interviews. The best strategy is to always be truthful about your background.

Hiring managers have love–hate relationships with resumés. They need resumés to find job seekers to fill job openings, but they often have to wade through piles of poorly written work histories. If you give a hiring manager the information needed to make a quick decision about your credentials, you will have an edge over other applicants.

## THE TOOLS YOU'LL NEED

Put together properly, the telephone script, the cover letter and the resumé are the 1-2-3 of scoring an interview. And that's when the real work starts.

## CASE STUDY
## From Secretary to Business Owner:
## Nan, 50

The turning point in Nan's life came when she went to the bank only to find her estranged husband had cleaned out their joint account. She had fifteen cents in her purse and three sons (aged nine months, three and a half years and six years) to support.

'I knew then if I didn't take charge of my life I would never get out of the downward spiral,' she recalled. Just over 21 years later, as she drove down the main street of Brisbane in a luxury car she had bought herself 'as a farewell gift', Nan could look back and reflect on just how far she had come.

Nan left school in 1967 at a time when the options for female school leavers were, as she puts it, 'not crash hot'. 'You either went into nursing, teaching or the public service,' she said. 'The main thing employers were interested in was how soon you were going to get married, have children and leave.'

Nan went to technical college and completed a secretarial course, learning shorthand and bookkeeping. She was then employed in the Sydney head office of a mining company where she rose to the position of personal assistant to the chairman. With the company executives often travelling to inspect the company's mines and holdings, Nan would run the office in their absence. At 21 she married, and had her first son at 22.

'My husband was in the hotel business and I joined him,' she said. 'He would manage the hotels and I would handle the front office. I would organise the functions, do the payroll and hiring and firing and bookkeeping. I found I read people well and enjoyed the personal side of the business.'

Nan had given birth to their second son and was pregnant with their third when her husband told her he was having an affair and their marriage was over. She left with the children and took the only job she could find –

as cleaner at a hotel run by a friend. 'In the space of a few months I had gone from running a hotel to scrubbing the toilets at one,' she said.

Another friend, a Holy Spirit nun, offered Nan a lifeline. 'She told me I could live on the grounds of a Holy Spirit convent in Brisbane,' she said. 'I had a house for me and my boys for $15 a week.'

It was soon after moving to Brisbane that Nan had what she calls her 'life-defining moment' at the bank. She joined a queue to apply for the Government deserted wife's pension and to take a refresher course in secretarial skills. Then she saw a newspaper advertisement announcing that a new company in Brisbane was looking for a secretary.

'It got down to being between me and a former Miss Australia,' Nan laughed. 'And I got the job.'

The company was a consulting firm, developing a niche market in Queensland. As she had in both the mining and hotel industries, Nan proved she had a natural aptitude for the work.

When the manager asked Nan to place an advertisement in the newspaper to employ another consultant, Nan told him that she could do the job. He gave her the opportunity to prove herself. Within eighteen months the manager had been transferred and Nan was promoted to run the Queensland operation. The business grew, and so did Nan's responsibilities.

'How did I know I could do everything that came my way?' she asks. 'I didn't. I just worked five times as hard as anyone else until I had mastered the job. I wasn't university educated, but I did have a good work ethic and I was determined to achieve results.'

Some ten years later head office told Nan that her division of the company was for sale. She and a fellow executive mounted a management buyout. In November 1990 when they took over the operation had a turnover of $1.5 million. By 1999 it had grown to $23 million. In August 1999 Nan and her partner sold their business to a large international organisation, staying on to run the company on a two-year contract.

When the time came to leave, Nan was financially secure, her three boys had grown into successful young men and she had well and truly achieved her dream career.

I knew the time was right to step aside, but I also know I have a lot more to do. I think if what I have achieved in my working life proves anything it is that if you really love what you are doing you will have a sense of purpose and once you have that you can do anything. When I think back on where I was 21 years ago, sometimes I can't believe it. As the time to leave my company came closer I saw a very beautiful motor vehicle and promised to buy it for myself as a parting gift. As I drove it from the showroom through town I just couldn't help thinking 'I wonder what those nuns would say if they could see me now!'

# 7
# the interview

For some people it is akin to undergoing root canal treatment. Others find it a breeze. Either way, one thing is certain, at some stage during your career you will have to undergo an interview. And, much as some like to underplay its importance, the fact is in most cases it is the most vital part of the entire employment process. Whether applying for your first job, changing positions or changing career direction, the interview is a major link in the chain. To put it brutally: mess up the interview and you have lost all hope of taking that next step.

So what is the interview all about? What is the best way to approach it and what do interviewers look for? One of our top young interviewers is head of a legal team in Sydney, interviewing and placing lawyers in positions with leading firms around the world. Some lawyers will be simply changing firms, others changing the direction of their careers and, in turn, their lives. As a lawyer himself, now involved in career consulting, his job history provides a prime example of the ongoing evolution that constitutes a person's career. He is often the first person that people speak to after they have decided to take the big step towards a career change. How they relate to him and the interview process could determine the future direction their lives take.

## FIRST IMPRESSIONS

First impressions are extremely important in the interview situation, and his advice is to do your best to make a good impression. Although it is only natural for people to respond at the outset to the more superficial issues of a person's presentation, it is the professional interviewer's job to uncover the facts related to the job seeker's competence.

> I can have a positive or negative reaction within the first
> thirty seconds. Obviously I am aware that some people
> are simply not comfortable in an interview and this
> should not be held against them, but the interviewer
> has to look at the job seeker through the eyes of the
> potential employer. One has to make an early assess-
> ment. If the job seeker does not impress me, chances
> are the employer will not be impressed either.

To that end, interviewers look for small but extremely telling signs. Whether the interviewee stands up as the interviewer enters the room. Whether they look the interviewer in the eye and give a firm handshake. Whether they are well presented. This is described as 'being focussed on the moment'. 'This is a key moment in that person's life. I need to see that they are treating the interview with the respect it deserves.'

## THE DO'S AND DON'TS

These then are the do's of being interviewed. The don'ts are equally clear cut.

'I don't want to see people who appear idle in their minds,' says one of our interviewers. 'Some that I have interviewed look like they have somewhere better to be. They are slumped in their chairs. There is no energy, no positivity, as if the interview is something they are being forced to endure. The question that immediately enters my mind is if they are half-hearted about the process, will they be half-hearted about the job?'

Then there is the important question of 'the fit'. Will this person be a cultural fit for the organisation? To this end interviewers are looking for appropriate presentation and dress.

These points may seem obvious, nevertheless he has seen his share of bad examples. He recalls:

Once I walked into the interview room and there was the job seeker head down, speaking on a mobile phone and going through some figures he had pulled out of his briefcase. He didn't look up, just raised a hand to signal that I shouldn't interrupt. He kept me waiting several minutes while he finished his call.

Another time I walked in and the job seeker had his feet on the table, reading a two-day-old newspaper he had brought with him. He didn't get up.

I also interviewed a lawyer for a position in a blue-chip law firm who was wearing a cardigan and Hush Puppies. While dress and presentation are issues of personal taste, the truth of the matter is that top firms have a certain style. If you do not meet that style, you are unlikely to fit into the culture of the organisation and it is usually a waste of everyone's time to proceed to the next step. I'm not saying everyone should try to look alike or that one style fits all. A person with body piercing and a red mohawk will look as out of place in some environments as a three-piece suit will in others. The potential employee is looking for a perfect fit. What that fit is differs in each case.

Basically, what the interviewer is looking for is a rapport with the job seeker. A successful interview should feel like a chat, a friendly discussion between two individuals. 'A good interviewer will make the job seeker feel at ease. We ideally work on a 20:80 ratio: 20 per cent of information coming from us, gathering 80 per cent of the information from them.'

With this in mind it is easy to see that some of the best interviewers are also the quietest. They don't monopolise the conversation, instead encouraging the job seeker to speak openly with some choice questions and words of encouragement. For this, after all, is what the interview is all about: to find out who the job seeker is, what they can do and where they can best do it.

While all interviews are different, and all interviewers have their own style, a typical interview with a recruitment agency will go something like this. In most cases, the job seeker will have approached the consulting firm in one of two ways. Either they will have lodged their resumé in the hope of making a change in their career, or they will have answered an advertisement. If the latter is the case, the consultant will have gone through all the replies, plus conducted a data search to see if any suitable applicants are already on the books. Let's say that fifty replies to the advertisement were received. Of these around twenty might be considered suitable. Another three could be added from the database of previous applicants, which all recruitment specialists have.

The consultant would then contact the selected twenty-three for what is called the 'pre-qualifying process'. Based on a telephone interview, the number would then be cut to anything from eight to twelve for face-to-face interviews. After the interviews a short list of five or six would be graded in order of priority and sent on to the client. The client may then ask to meet with one, two or even all six applicants. In some cases the consultant will sit in on the interviews.

The client will then make the final choice. The consultant should ask for the reasons the other job seekers were not successful and pass this information on to them. Their names would be added to the database and, when a suitable position becomes available, they would be contacted.

This seems a very cut-and-dried process, but of course as with anything in which human contact is involved, there are variables. And this is where the skill and empathy of the interviewer comes to the fore. The ability to make the applicant feel at ease is paramount, says our interviewer.

> For the first few minutes I will attempt to build a rapport, to try to make the applicant feel comfortable enough to discuss sensitive issues, such as salaries, or why they are upset in their current environment. Even there, you can learn a lot. Sometimes people will start ranting and raving about their current employer, demonstrating negativity. Sometimes they are downright bitchy. That quickly gives an insight into their personality. In other cases they will actually be traumatised, disturbed about their job. In those cases my job is about being a good listener. You virtually have to be a counsellor. Of course, I will always know a little bit about the person I am interviewing because they will have forwarded their resumé and, while I will have acquainted myself with the resumé, it is really only a starting point. I will attempt to have the applicant add value to the resumé. It is not always easy. Sometimes there is simply no rapport. People will come in and say 'Here's my resumé, I want a job in

such and such a firm, I have a meeting in ten minutes,
so what information do you need?'

In those cases it is about time management, getting the information and trying to help the person achieve their goal.

To do that you have to unlock the doors that will lead to
four key elements. You must find out about the
individual, find what they want to do and whether they
are suited to it, find the environment they are suited to,
and find the rewards they will be happy with, both
financial and social. Once you have that information
you are then able to make a match between what
someone wants and what is available to them.

Just as there are keys to being a successful interviewer, there
are keys to being a successful interviewee.

- First, be attentive and a good listener. If you talk at the
  interviewer rather than with him or her, they will conclude
  that you could find it hard to integrate into an established
  team environment.
- Take the opportunity to promote yourself and your skills,
  but do not overstep the mark and appear egotistical.
- Give a sense of what you are capable of. If you want to move
  into a new area, show that you have the capabilities needed
  for the move. If you wish to make a complete change of
  direction in order to follow your dream, show a commitment to that dream. If you want to be a rocket scientist,
  be prepared to list your achievements as a physicist and your
  membership of a hobby rocket club. If you want to enter
  the film industry, have some amateur videos and a list of
  reviews and awards under your arm.

- You will need to understand your own resumé and be able to talk in detail about everything listed on it.

- Tell the truth. Don't overstate your involvement in a project or campaign – a good interviewer will find you out, either through a few well-chosen questions or by checking your references. Just because you walked past a room when a project was being discussed does not make you part of that project.

- Talk about your mistakes! Yes, this leads them to an incident you are familiar with, as well as showing that you are able to learn and have the humility to admit to not being perfect.

- Likewise, be careful not to 'forget' to list all employers. One long period of employment with one employer might look better than three or even four short ones but again, a reference check will find you out.

- On the other hand, if you have achieved something, don't let modesty stop you from talking about it. If you have had a big win, give the details in a concise, methodical manner. The project was X, the outcome was Y.

- Do not try to ingratiate yourself with the interviewer. They don't have to like you, just to be confident that you can do the job.

Do all that and you will get the job, right? Well, unfortunately it is not that easy. Sometimes the applicant might come across perfectly at the interview, but the resumé does not look good. In those cases the consultant may ask the client to look beyond the piece of paper. In other cases, no matter how hard the applicant tries to follow the golden rules, they just don't perform well in the interview. One of our interviewers has encountered this situation many times and will take extreme measures if he feels the applicant has what it takes.

There have been times when I've had to go back to an applicant and say 'Look, your experience is great, your work ethic is great, everything about you is great, but there is no way you are going to get this position because you simply don't come across well at interview.' I tell them if they are willing to give it a try I will put them through a mock interview and coach them about how to show the client what they really have to offer. I will spend a few hours, pretending to be the client and most times I can turn them around. It might just be a case of articulating their answers, overcoming shyness or modesty. Even just expanding on what they have to say rather than giving one-word or two-word answers. Their posture could be poor, they might slump in their chair or not look the interviewer in the eye. It could be a case of inappropriate dress or even personal hygiene. Sometimes it is hard, but you have to be brutally honest and tell the applicant they have a body-odour problem that could be easily fixed. These are just small issues that are getting in the way of the main game – the fact that the applicant would be a perfect fit for the employer if he or she could just get their message across.

If the applicant still doesn't get the opportunity to take that step along the path towards the dream career, it is really just a matter of time until the perfect match comes along. It is just a case of sticking at it. The person wanting to make a change in their career might think getting through the interview is like swimming across a swamp full of crocodiles. In fact, if handled successfully, it is the bridge across to the other side.

## HOW TO IMPROVE YOUR PERFORMANCE AT INTERVIEWS

*All applicants undertaking an interview at our company are given access to this guide to interviews. Available in waiting rooms, the guide gives applicants an insight into what they can expect, and how to make the most of the interview opportunity.*

The approach you take at a job interview could have a dramatic effect on your career prospects. It is therefore important that you perform well because, no matter how good your career is to date, the employment interview remains an important step towards achievement of your ambitions. These suggestions will assist you to perform confidently and effectively in interviews with prospective employers.

### Preparation for the interview

Preparation is the essential first step towards a successful interview.

* Know the exact place and time of the interview, the interviewer's full name, its correct pronunciation and his/her title.
* Find out specific facts about the company: where its offices, plants or stores are located; what its products and services are; what its growth has been; and what its growth potential is for the future. Most organisations now have a web site that provides much of this information. Have a look at the company's research publications in hard copy or via the Internet.
* Refresh your memory on the facts and figures of your present employer and former employers. You will be expected to know a lot about a company for which you have previously worked. Pay particular attention to how you will describe your most important achievements.

- Prepare the questions you will ask during the interview. Remember that an interview is a two-way street. The employer will try to determine through questioning if you have the qualifications necessary to do the job. You must determine through questioning whether the company will give you the opportunity for the growth and development you seek. Here are some of the probing questions you might want to ask:
  - May I have a detailed description of the position?
  - Why has the position become available?
  - What is the culture of the company?
  - Is there an induction and training program?
  - What sort of people have done well in the company?
  - Are there advanced training programs for those who demonstrate outstanding ability?
  - How would my success be measured in this role?
  - What are the earnings of those successful people in their third year?
  - What are the company's plans for growth?
  - What are the best-selling products or services?
  - What is the next step?
- Dress conservatively. Pay attention to all facets of your dress and grooming.
- Be prepared with answers and supporting examples to questions such as:
  - What are your career aspirations?
  - Why would you like to work for our organisation?
  - What was your last salary and bonus?
  - What style of management gets the best from you?
  - What interests you about our products and services?
  - Can you get recommendations from previous employers?
  - What would they say about you?

- What have you learned from some of your jobs? Which did you enjoy most? Why?
- What have you done which shows initiative in your career?
- What are the key skills you need to develop further? What are you doing about these?
- What do you think determines a person's progress in a good company?
- Are you willing to relocate?
- How do you spend your spare time? What are your hobbies?
- What does teamwork mean to you?
- What entrepreneurial activities have you been engaged in?
- Have you saved previous employers money or resources?

- Be prepared for the use of competency-based questions as part of the interview. These are currently a common practice. You may need to provide concrete examples that demonstrate you have the core competencies required for the role (e.g. leadership, achieving sales budgets, team management or database management). If, for example, the interviewer is looking for someone who is a strategic thinker, you may be asked:
  - Can you describe a strategy that you have devised and implemented for your organisation?
  - What was the outcome?

## What the interviewer is looking for

During the course of an interview, the interviewer will be evaluating your total performance, not just your answers. Listed below are some factors that will usually produce a positive reaction from a prospective employer:

- Interested, balanced approach.
- Ability to express thoughts clearly.
- Evidence of career planning and objective setting.
- Confidence and enthusiasm.

- Informative replies.
- Tact, maturity and courtesy.
- Maintenance of eye contact.
- Positive handshake.
- Intelligent questions about the job.
- Preparation and knowledge of the company/industry.
- Evidence of flexibility and ability to handle change.

## The interview

You are being interviewed because the interviewer wants to hire somebody – not because they want to trip up or embarrass you.

### Interview Do's and Don'ts

1. DO plan to arrive early. Allow for traffic delays or rain. Late arrival for a job interview is never excusable.
2. If presented with an application, DO fill it out neatly and completely. Be sure the person you give your resumé to is the person who will actually do the hiring.
3. DO greet the interviewer by his/her surname if you are sure of the pronunciation. If not, ask them to repeat it.
4. DO shake hands firmly.
5. DO wait until you are offered a chair before sitting. Sit upright in your chair. Look alert and interested at all times. Be a good listener as well as a good talker. Smile.
6. DO maintain good eye contact.
7. DO follow the interviewer's leads, but try to get the interviewer to describe the position and the duties to you early in the interview so that you can relate your background and skills to the position.

8.  DON'T answer questions with a simple 'yes' or 'no'. Explain whenever possible. Tell those things about yourself that relate to the position.

9.  DO make sure that your good points get across to the interviewer in a factual, sincere manner. Keep in mind that you alone can sell yourself to an interviewer. Make them realise the need for you in their organisation.

10. DO be honest. Answer all questions truthfully, frankly and as much to the point as possible.

11. DON'T ever make derogatory remarks about your present or former employers or companies.

12. DON'T 'over-answer' questions. The interviewer may steer the conversation into politics or economics. Since this can be ticklish, it is best to answer the questions honestly, trying not to say more than is necessary.

13. If you get the impression that the interview is not going well and that you have already been rejected, DON'T let your discouragement show. Once in a while an interviewer who is genuinely interested in your possibilities may strongly challenge your weaknesses in order to test your reaction. Remain positive and DON'T become defensive.

14. DON'T inquire about salary, holidays, bonuses, etc. at the initial interview unless you are positive the employer is interested in hiring you and raises the issue first. However, you should know your market value and be prepared to specify your required salary or range.

15. DO always conduct yourself as if you are determined to get the job you are discussing. Never close the door on an opportunity. It is better to be in the position where you can choose from a number of jobs rather than only one.

Through the interaction that takes place during the interview, the interviewer will be searching for your strong and weak points, evaluating your qualifications, skills and intellectual qualities and they will probably probe deeply to determine your attitudes, aptitudes, stability, motivation and maturity.

## Closing the interview

- If you are interested in the position, restate your interest and ask what the next step is. If you are offered the position and you need some time to think it over, be courteous and tactful in asking for that time. Set a definite date when you can provide an answer.

- Don't be too discouraged if no definite offer is made or specific salary discussed. The interviewer will probably want to communicate with their office first or interview more applicants before making a decision.

- Thank the interviewer for their time and consideration of you for the position. You have done all you can if you have answered the two questions uppermost in his or her mind:
  1. Why are you interested in the job and the company?
  2. What can you offer and can you do the job?

## After the interview

If you have been referred by a consultant, the first thing you should do is call the consultant immediately after the interview and discuss what happened. The consultant will want to talk to you before the interviewer calls them. If you are interested in progressing further, your consultant will assist. They will want to know your feelings, together with your perception of what the interviewer's reaction is likely to be.

Finally, *relax* – you have done all you can.

**CASE STUDY**
**From Lawyer to Executive Recruiter:**
**Jason, 30**

Jason left school with big dreams and a firm idea of the best way to achieve them. He entered university to study economics and law with the ambition of becoming a CEO of a large firm. As Jason progressed through his studies he found himself drawn to the legal side of his course and ultimately found himself working with arguably the country's premier legal firm. For six years Jason immersed himself in a legal career, to the exclusion of all else.

'I would regularly work fourteen-hour days, often on dry, technical work which wore me out and drained much of my personality and energy,' he recalled. 'Ultimately, it was clear to me that the life of a corporate lawyer was not for me. I needed a radical change in my career. I knew that I could make a valuable contribution to the right career, but just needed to find my thing.'

His realisation that his career lay outside the strictures of a law firm came as a relief. He took an analytical approach in order to find a new direction.

'I considered my strengths and identified that I thrived on business development, transactional work and human interaction. I liked autonomy and liked performance-based remuneration. Interestingly, none of these featured prominently in my career as a lawyer.'

Jason narrowed his options down to property development and executive recruitment.

'I had a passion for property development, but felt inclined to utilise my legal networks and knowledge more directly,' he said. 'I had met a few recruiters, each of whom I respected. They all enjoyed their careers. Upon further investigation, my interest in pursuing a career as a recruiter increased.'

He felt that rather than approaching recruitment firms and asking how they could help him, he would tell them how he could help them. With strong contacts in the legal profession and an insider's knowledge of how the profession worked, he was proactive, offering himself and his expertise as a 'package deal'.

'Having researched the recruitment market, I approached two international recruitment firms with a business plan to start-up a legal recruitment business for them,' he said. 'Both firms registered immediate interest and commenced a process involving multiple interviews and, for one firm, psychometric tests.'

Jason began his new career three years ago and, as he says, the ride has been amazing.

The business, and my career with it, grew around me. The team grew from two people (including me) to become Australasia's premier legal recruitment business with twenty-eight consultants across Australia and New Zealand. My role, as manager of the Australasian legal business provides an incredibly diverse and stimulating career involving significant PR, marketing, strategic direction and management.

Jason has no regrets. By using his university training and practical experience and transferring them into a new field, he has achieved a perfect career move. He has, in effect, taken the elements of law that he enjoyed, and placed them in an environment to which he is better suited. While remuneration wasn't a primary motivation in making the move, it has been a pleasant consequence.

The change, although radical at the time, is the best career decision I ever made. The move into a new area was a risk and involved a great leap of faith. But it worked. I discovered a business that suited me perfectly. I now get up each day excited about the challenges ahead, very different to some of the dreary starts that I had as a lawyer. It is a pleasant benefit that my earnings have consistently outstripped my expectations and the earnings of my peers still slogging it out as lawyers.

My girlfriend at the time encouraged me to follow my heart because she could see that I was stifled in my role as a lawyer. With my career shift, she saw an incredible change in my demeanour. In addition, I reduced my average working day to eleven or twelve hours a day – working those hours by choice as I enjoyed the work and could see the fruits of every additional hour that I spent developing the business.

# 8

# high-tech interviewing

If the thought of sitting in an office in front of a panel of inter-viewers and being given the third-degree is your worst nightmare, think again. The IT age has opened up a whole set of new ways to make you feel uncomfortable! How about sitting in front of a panel of interviewers who you can see only on a television screen? Or answering multiple-choice behavioural questions on your computer knowing that one wrong answer will cut you from the list before you even get to the interview? Or being interviewed through e-mail or on video . . . the possibilities are endless.

Once again, technology has taken us into a new dimension, and it's not the Twilight Zone. Not quite, but for anyone who is uncomfortable in an interview situation (and isn't that just about everyone?) it is close.

## VIDEOCONFERENCE INTERVIEWS

Writing on Monster.com about videoconference interviews, interview specialist Carole Martin gave the example of Craig S., who was questioned by interviewers in New York City and Japan, simultaneously, without ever leaving his home in Minnesota.

Employers can now see and judge appearance and body language to get a deeper sense of what applicants have to offer before flying them cross-country for interviews. This includes the capability of viewing applicants at multiple sites, in various States and countries, at the same time. When Craig learned he was being considered for the position of business development manager for a Fortune 500 company, he was ecstatic. And then he heard the bad news: he would have to fly to Texas within the week. Craig was unable to travel due to work commitments, and since the committee of interviewers had a targeted date to narrow their search, it looked like Craig was out of the running. But, thanks to technology, he was offered another option: an interview by videoconference.

The company set up the process and managed the details. All Craig had to do was drive to a location some fifty kilometres away from his home. Within minutes of his arrival, he was being interviewed by people in New York City and Japan. Craig was groomed and prepared and did well in the interview. He was now placed among the three finalists. They were ready to accommodate his schedule and fly him to Texas.

Videoconferencing is not a substitute for a face-to-face interview, and a personal meeting would always be the first preference, but the advantages sometimes outweigh the disadvantages. This technology saves time, money and allows several locations to connect at once, in spite of major time differences. This type of interviewing is gaining in popularity as technology improves. It will only be a matter of time before you can sit in your own home

## Carole's Videoconference Interview Pointers

- Speak up if you're experiencing any difficulty with sound, delays or picture. This is not a time to suffer in silence. It will not be held against you if the technology is not working in your favour.

- Dress conservatively in solid colours. Keep distractions like jewellery to a minimum. Choose soft, neutral shades rather than black and white, which are too extreme on camera. Various shades of blue work well. Watch TV presenters and newscasters for other ideas of what might look good on camera.

- Look at the camera full-face, as though you were presenting the news. Talk to the camera as you would to any person interviewing you. Be conversational and maintain eye contact and be sure to smile.

- Keep your movements limited. Hand gestures will be magnified on the screen. While arms waving about can be distracting, you don't want to look stiff either. Use small, smooth movements when gesturing.

- At the same time, forget about the camera and the technology. Focus on your purpose and presentation. You want the attention and concentration to be on you and what you are saying.

- Be aware that there is a lag in transmission as data is compressed and sent from one location to another. This means there will be a silence while you sit and wait for a response from the other end. Some interviewees find this works to their advantage, because they can actually watch the interviewers while their answers to the interviewers' questions are received. The trick, which will become obvious, is not to step on the other person's words. Allow for the delay.

or office and be interviewed around the world. So Carole's final advice is: 'The future of interviewing is nearly here. Be prepared.'

## HIGH-TECH INTERVIEWING TECHNIQUES

The future is already here. More and more organisations are using technology to make interviewing less expensive, while simultaneously casting a wide geographic net to attract a global pool of job seekers. It makes sense from a company standpoint, though for the job seeker it throws some additional complexity into an already stressful process. The three common methods of high-tech interviewing are:

- *E-mail interview*

  An e-mail interview, or one through instant messaging, is sometimes used as an initial step in the hiring process. It can be difficult since you are not face to face with your interviewer. The best thing you can do is to err on the side of formality: don't be too chatty, keep the 'dialogue' professional, but try to build some rapport by using the interviewer's name and information you know about the organisation. Usually, you will not be offered a job without at least a telephone interview or a face-to-face meeting following an e-chat.

- *Video interview*

  Video interviews can be challenging for several reasons. If done with an overseas office, the time difference can throw you if the interview is either very early in the morning or late at night. Technical difficulties can shake your composure and if the talking is not synchronised with facial expressions – even if off by only a second – this can make you feel unnatural and add to the stress. To put your best foot forward, prepare as you would for any interview. Don't keep notes any place that would cause you to read from them. Be aware of the importance of looking into the lens ('eye contact'), smile, and do your best to simulate a conversation with someone (imagining you are talking to someone across a desk can be helpful). Be sure not to run on too long. This can be deadly on videotape when that fast-forward button is available.

- *Telephone interview*

  Telephone interviews have been used for a long time, though increasingly they are happening internationally. Generally, the big advantage of being evaluated over the phone is that you can have notes in front of you to help you remember important examples of accomplishments you want to mention. The downside is that you risk becoming dependent upon them and sounding 'canned'. Over the phone and without the benefit of body language, there is more of a burden to develop a strong rapport. Make a conscious effort to remain upbeat, focussed, ask good questions and use the interviewer's name when appropriate.

'Remember,' says one of our international career experts, 'an interview is a positive step in the hiring process. You have made it through the paper cut and now have the opportunity to articulate your credentials and enthusiasm. New interview techniques simply require a bit of additional preparation to enhance your comfort level, so that you put your best foot forward.'

## Tips for High-Tech Interviews

- Preparation is still the most important step. This hasn't changed. You need to be able to succinctly articulate your strengths, work background, interest in the job and organisation, your commitment to the career field, and your goals for the future.

You also need to do your homework on the organisation and the job. There is plenty of interviewing material that is well-written and can help you with your preparation. Monster.com provides excellent interview information as well as a virtual interviewing centre. Simply click on 'Select Virtual Interview'.

- Practice is critical. You should anticipate five to ten questions that you might be asked and practise answering them in front of a mirror, with a friend or colleague, or simply quietly on your own. By having a sense of what might be asked and knowing the important points you want to make, you will be more relaxed, which can only help your cause. To practise tough questions go to interview.Monster.com and click on 'Rehearsal'.
- Follow-up is critical, but often ignored. Send a thank-you note within forty-eight hours if possible, then call or e-mail if you don't hear anything, either a few days after you were expecting to hear, or within ten days if you didn't know when you might be contacted. This shows professionalism, interest, and commitment.

## NARROWING THE FIELD

Another expert writer warns that the IT explosion has led to one more hurdle that candidates-to-be may have to overcome before they even get to be considered candidates: the pre-screened computer interview – an online question-and-answer session aimed at narrowing the field.

These have been around for a few years, but more companies are using them as a time-saver to weed out unsuitable job seekers. The reasoning is simple: Why waste precious time interviewing a pack of job seekers when you can weed out the undesirables by using a comprehensive online interview?

For example, US-based information services company EDS calls its questionnaire the 'first step of our new developmental recruiting process'. EDS has an entire web site devoted to pre-screening potential candidates. Before an interviewer even shakes your hand, he or she knows all about you: your employment history, and, most importantly, whether you're a team player, problem-solver or potential fast-tracker.

EDS's online interview is not something you can knock out while watching TV. You need at least forty-five minutes to answer a barrage of questions such as:

1. Would you rather have structure or flexibility in your job?
2. How often do you forget important details?
3. How often do your decisions have unexpected consequences?
4. In the past, what approach have you chosen to solve difficult problems?
5. How would you react to working without direct supervision, setting your own goals and meeting them?
6. In what type of work environment are you most productive?
7. In the past, when you have been assigned numerous tasks with little direction, how did you react?

Punch in the wrong response and you'll never hear from your dream company. 'But, determining so-called right and wrong answers is not so simple,' says Brian Stern, a psychologist and managing director of a US-based HR consulting company. Most job seekers deem a right answer to be what they think a company wants to hear and a wrong answer just the opposite. But, it doesn't work that way, says Brian, who designs hundreds of questionnaires for different jobs that range from production supervisors to CEOs. Stern thinks the pre-assessment technique is the way of the future because it 'casts a wide net' and hauls in those who are qualified. He estimates about a quarter of job seekers in the US get jobs as a result of this process.

How do you succeed with these tricky assessment interviews? Believe it or not, it's done by not telling companies what they want to hear, but by simply being honest, says Brian.

How would you answer the following questions?

- *In the past, what approach have you chosen to solve difficult problems?*
  1. I have thoroughly investigated all aspects of the job.
  2. I have felt overwhelmed and asked someone for help.
  3. I have requested guidance from my supervisor or professor to find the solution.
  4. I have given up and moved on to a new task.
  5. I don't know.
- *How do you feel about making unpopular decisions?*
  1. I like to make decisions I know will be unpopular.
  2. I have no problem making unpopular decisions.
  3. I don't like to make unpopular decisions, but I can if necessary.
  4. I prefer not to make unpopular decisions.
  5. I can't make unpopular decisions.
  6. I have never made an unpopular decision.

Most people would pick '1.' for the first question and '2.' for the second. But they could be making a big mistake. Why? Because, says Brian, 'Companies are looking for a good fit by fitting jobs to people.' They identify traits for a particular job, such as project manager or systems analyst, and then try to find people with matching traits. In the first question, for example, the job may not require someone who stays with a problem until doomsday, but someone who asks for help and moves to the next problem. In the second one, the company may be looking for a manager who can build rapport. Number 3 might be the answer they are looking for.

'It's important to be candid,' Brian says. 'There are trap questions that are designed to see if you are responding in an overly socially responsible manner.' In a word, fudging. 'The last thing you want to do is paint a picture that's not you.'

## THE INTERVIEWING PANEL

Even if you survive the computerised screening process or high-tech interviewing techniques, eventually you will have to come face to face with another human. But don't assume that is always going to be straightforward. Another stressful form of interview sometimes used is the multiple interview, where the applicant must face a panel, a board or an interviewing team. Daunting as this might seem, there is an upside. You would probably have to face all these people at some stage in the interview process anyway. At least this way you are getting it all over at once.

But how do you deal with so many interviewers in one sitting? The best way is to take them one at a time.

The board or panel is not one entity, but several individuals coming together with the common goal of hiring the best candidate for the job. At the same time, each person has his own agenda or department's interest at heart. For example, the HR manager will be checking to make sure you are a good fit with the culture and people working at this company. The hiring manager will want to know about your technical skills or business know-how. And the person from accounting will want to know if you are savvy enough to operate a business budget. Board or panel interviews are usually rather formal and organised, using a standard set of questions for all applicants. This type of interview is typically used in academia, government or for high-level executives, but can be used for any other type of position in any company.

Take the example of a woman interviewed for a senior administrative job at a major health agency, facing a panel of ten doctors, nurses, technicians and administrators. She felt like it was an inquisition, not an interview. But she had prepared well and was confident when she faced this tribunal. She looked at each person as he or she asked the question, and continued to look at that person for 30 seconds or so. She then shifted her eye contact to each member of the interviewing team. She made sure she made contact with each set of eyes while answering questions. She felt very much in control and her interview went well. The result was a job offer.

Carole Martin describes another multiple-type interview as the 'good cop–bad cop' interview. The team is usually made up of two interviewers, one who asks the questions and one who takes notes. The two typically trade roles, which can be confusing if they have different styles. In fact, one person may be kind and gentle and the other more abrupt or pushy. Her advice? Just remember, these inquisitors are working together toward the same end. Treat them equally, not favouring one over the other.

Regardless of the type of interview, the best advice is to prepare and practise beforehand. When you have your script and have rehearsed your answers, you will feel prepared and more confident no matter how many people you have to face. Lastly, a good tip to remember is to make sure you get each person's business card, hopefully at the beginning of the interview, so you can address each person by name. If you have a pad and pen on your lap, quickly draw a diagram, showing where each of the interviewers sits, and their name. Refer to it quickly when answering questions, so that you can use the names. The interviewers might realise what you have done, but chances are they will admire your initiative.

## THE BEHAVIOURAL INTERVIEW

Which brings us to another potentially intimidating interview process: the behavioural interview. When asking behavioural questions, the interviewer is listening for specific examples of how you have handled situations or problems in the past. Behavioural questions begin with phrases like 'Tell me about a time when . . .' or 'Can you give me an example of . . .' The interviewer wants to hear your real-life examples. When an interviewer asks such questions, he or she is listening for examples of how you handled situations similar to the ones you may handle for this company. According to Carole, this is your chance to talk about your accomplishments. If you can demonstrate, through examples, preferably recent, that you have succeeded in certain areas that are of interest, you will be considered a possible candidate for success in a future position. After all, if you did it somewhere else yesterday, you can do it for this company tomorrow. Your success stories should include the situation, the action you took and the result. Carole uses this example for someone interviewing for a sales position:

*The situation*: I had a customer who did not want to hear about the features of my merchandise because of a prior interaction with my company.
*The action*: I listened to her story and made sure I heard her complaint. I then explained how I would have handled the situation differently and how I can offer her better service. I showed her some facts that changed her mind about dealing with the company again.
*The result*: She not only bought the merchandise, but

complimented me on how I handled her account.

She is now one of my best customers.

You can prepare for this type of interview by writing out your stories before the interview. Determine what stories you have that would be appropriate for the position based on its job description. If the job requires dependability, write your story about a time when your dependability was recognised or made a difference with a customer.

You can use the stories you prepare even if the interviewer does not ask behavioural questions. If you are asked a traditional question, use your prepared story and preface it with, 'I can give you an example of a time when I used that skill on a previous job.' By preparing for the interview ahead of time and recalling your past successes, you will be able to have examples in mind and will not be caught off guard. There is no way you can predict what the interviewer is going to ask you, but you can prepare what you want him or her to know about your past as a predictor of your future performance.

Once you have an interview, whether it be face to face, through a video camera, via a computer or even over the telephone, just remember that the people you are communicating with want to fill the role as much as you want to be the person who fills it. If you are the right person, and you let them know that, you will be about to take the next step on the road to a dream career.

## CASE STUDY
### From Financial Institution to Sales and Marketing: Keith, 48

When he was 36 years old Keith saw his future clearly mapped out in front of him – and the view made him feel like screaming with frustration.

On the advice of his parents, who wanted a secure future for their son, Keith completed a commerce-based university degree. He then joined a financial institution on a graduate program. After fifteen years in the financial world, at the age of 36, he knew he had to get away – or he never would.

I knew if I didn't make a clean break I would be working there for the rest of my life and the prospect made me almost physically ill. My parents were right. It was a secure future, but it just wasn't right for me. I found the world of financial institutions stodgy and restrictive. After fifteen years I felt like I was putting on a straitjacket every time I got ready for work. I had joined the firm straight after graduating and felt like I had missed out on a lot of life's experiences.

In what was probably the most radical thing he had done in his adult life, Keith resigned from the firm and bought an open-ended ticket for Europe. He travelled for the next eighteen months and headed home ready to find another role for which he was better suited. Taking the skills he had acquired and most enjoyed over his years in the finance industry, such as strategic sales, customer relations and key account management, Keith was able to secure a position as a sales representative in the publishing industry, a world that excited and interested him.

Over the next ten years Keith worked his way through the company, before a downsizing saw him retrenched.

I was disappointed, of course, and it was a little frightening because I now had a wife and children to consider. But I had seen how the skills I learnt in my first job had enabled me to succeed in my second job. I was hopeful that I could find something else that would combine everything I had picked up along the way. I re-entered the employment market seeing it as an opportunity rather than a derailment.

Keith's positive attitude paid dividends. Once again he was able to find a job that used key skills he had acquired over the previous twenty-five years. Combining his financial background and literary background, he secured a key role in an e-learning company.

I think the most important thing I learnt along the way was how to be an effective networker. I had managed to maintain contact with a variety of people I had met in my work. I kept in touch with them, built up relationships and when I was retrenched I was able to find out pretty quickly what was available and what was open to me.

My current role is again exciting. It is the future of publishing and to be able to get involved at such an important stage in the industry's development is very stimulating. I get up in the morning wanting to get in to work. It is a far cry from where I was twenty years ago. I hate to think where I would be now if I hadn't made the move back then. Actually, I do know where I would be: sitting back at the same desk doing the same type of work. The decision to walk away from that world seemed very difficult at the time, but now I can look back at it as the best move I ever made.

# 9

# show me the money

Money should never be the sole motivating force behind a change in direction. To many people it is important, but it should be no more important than the pursuit of happiness and contentment in a work environment. As we have said before, money is not what makes the dream job, it is a consequence of having the dream job. If you are doing what you want to do, and doing it well, money will probably follow. Be warned though: it doesn't always come quickly. Sometimes, in order to make a change in direction towards a more suitable job, you may have to earn less money than you do currently. This must be weighed up against a whole raft of considerations. You must decide how much you really want to change, and how much you are willing to invest – both emotionally and financially – in order to make that change. You cannot compare money to happiness, but you can work out your sums and decide, down to the last cent, how much of a cut in salary you can afford to take if you have to. If you are a well-paid professional, bored by your job but also with a family, a large mortgage and enormous outgoings each month, obviously your potential for change is less than a homebody whose major extravagance is a takeaway pizza and video every week. Weigh up your options carefully. If the sums add up, the next step is to go out and explore the market.

## HOW MUCH AM I WORTH?

If you are simply moving from one position to another in the same field or industry you will, no doubt, have a fair idea of the type of remuneration package applicable to the position you are aiming at. If the field is something entirely foreign to you, you will need to do some research. Either way, you should know the range of money and conditions that is feasible and acceptable. As we said, money shouldn't be the main objective. It is far better to try to find a job in which you will be challenged, comfortable and happy. But in saying that, never undersell yourself. It is our experience that if you think that your employer is underpaying, or even exploiting you, you won't stay challenged, comfortable or happy for long.

Which brings us to the bottom line: how much are you worth, and how do you get it? Money is a sensitive issue and never more than when negotiating a salary package. Some people find it very difficult to discuss, others want to discuss it too much. Some people allow themselves to be underpaid; others will miss opportunities because they overvalue their services. So what is the correct etiquette when it comes to discussing money and conditions? When is the time to broach the subject?

> If your only career strategy is to wait until the headhunter calls or something new comes to you, how will you ever know what you are worth?

Well, certainly not the first time you sit down for an interview with a prospective employer. Yes, yes, we know. If the money is not right, you will not want the job, so why not? The fact is there is as much a protocol when it comes to applying for a job as there is to sitting down for a meal with your new employer. You wouldn't ask for the dessert menu before you ordered your entree. Neither should you ask about money before you both know whether you are going to be able to work together and, more importantly, know you are both serious about taking the next step.

Sometimes employers will use a job interview to test the waters or do some low-key market research about their firm and how it is viewed in the marketplace. They will want to know what you think of them, how much you are paid in your present position, so that they can compare this with their pay structure. This is sometimes also true of employees who will try to test the market and see what they are worth, whether their current employer is undervaluing them, or if they could earn more elsewhere. There is nothing wrong with this, it is good to know how much you are worth whether you are looking to change your place of employment or not, just as employers like to know how they are viewed in the marketplace. This, of course, is not to say you should just give this information freely, any more than the employer will want to give you a free look at the inner workings of their company. You should both know you are serious before you get down to the specifics of pay and conditions.

This does not mean you should go to the first interview with no idea of the range of salary the employer is expecting to pay. Ideally, if you have been advised correctly, you should only be applying for positions that are appropriate for you. First, of course, you will have a fair idea of what sort of salary package such a position will command. If you do not, there are various ways to find out. Do some research. If you have friends or contacts in the industry, ask for some anecdotal evidence. Look through the newspapers for several weeks to see what is on offer; visit a major employment web site, or call a leading recruitment firm with a specialisation in your area. Their experts will be pleased to offer you advice. You don't have to go into specifics about yourself and your current situation, but a general conversation should yield a good idea of the range of remuneration you would expect before you start the interview process.

Our career portal Monster.com offers a free guide to salaries and benefits for a necessarily limited selection of industries and professions. Depending on the country in which you wish to work, the form that this guide takes differs, but it is still possible to make a comparison. For instance, if you plan to work in Australia, go to Monster.com, click on the link to Australia, follow the prompts to 'Career Centre' and go to the 'Salary Centre' where you will find the 'Salary Calculator'. You will be asked to specify the city in which you are interested, the field and a title description. You will be given a range, usually varying by between \$10 000 and \$20 000. To compare this to the salary and benefits offered for a similar position in the USA, click on 'USA', go to 'Career Center' and you will find a guide to salary and benefits for 160 benchmark positions. Each of these positions, under a number of industry categories, is listed with an average minimum salary, average mean and average maximum. The guide will also show what sort of bonus an employee can expect. The system is similar for the UK page, which offers results of an extensive career survey. By doing some simple research on the Internet, you should be able to embark on your job search armed with a good idea of the range of salary and benefits attached to the position you desire.

Once you have that knowledge, only apply for positions offering the package you would accept. Again, there are a number of ways to determine whether a position is suitable. Most likely the job will be advertised with a published range of salary. If the advertisement does not mention a range, you should try to ascertain it as soon as possible. If the job has been advertised through a recruitment firm there should be a telephone number to ring for further information. It is quite acceptable to ring the consultant handling the position and ask what range of remuneration applies to the position. The consultant will be able to give you a broad range to let you know whether you are 'fighting in your weight division' (that is, it is not well above your experience or you are not overskilled for it).

If the job has been advertised directly through the employer or you have just been invited in on spec, perhaps after being recommended by a third party, you will have to broach the subject with the prospective employer. This should be done either during a phone call to confirm your appointment, or at the first interview. Again, for those who have a problem talking about money, there are ways around the situation. Never ask directly 'What does it pay?' Think of the interview process as the start of a meaningful relationship. The first interview is the first date. The best way to ask about the salary package is to say something like: 'Incidentally, what range of salary are we talking about here?' or 'Just to give me a sense of the type of package we are talking about, what range are you considering?' or best of all, if you have a good idea of the position and what you would consider acceptable: 'My expectation is X, is that feasible?'

All these questions are quite acceptable on the first date . . . make that, interview. The interviewer will be expecting it. If the right time has not presented itself, there will always be a time when the interviewer asks 'Do you have any questions?' This is definitely one of the questions he or she will be expecting.

Once the range has been established, the specific remuneration is the issue of sensitivity. This is where the game becomes more delicate and etiquette really comes into play. Never go into specifics at the first interview, unless the interviewer does. Again, remember that you do not want to divulge too much information about your present situation at this stage either. You want to know that both parties are serious before opening up too much. Talking specifics is only a 'maybe' at the second interview. You will just have to read the signals. If the interviewer seems completely comfortable, go with the flow, but don't push the issue yourself. By the third interview, it's time to go for it. You've both come this far, so there is definitely a chance that you both want to go all the way. Therefore, you want to know everything: base salary, super-annuation (in Australia there is a Government-set minimum, but some employers will pay more) and salary packaging (such things as company car, parking, health insurance and mobile phone bills). All these have to be calculated to see how they affect your pre-tax salary payments.

## NEGOTIATING THE SALARY PACKAGE

There are many different perks that can be included in a salary package, which can both make your professional life easier and lower your pre-tax earnings. These include:

* company car (we have heard of some organisations offering their top executives a car allowance that can be used to lease two cars, a small runabout to get to and from work, and a family vehicle)
* laptop computer
* mobile phone
* payment of home phone bills
* flight club membership
* professional memberships (such as industry clubs and organ-isations)
* gym membership

- personal trainer
- time and resources to facilitate relevant additional training and postgraduate studies
- travel allowances
- subsidised meals (both during and outside work hours)
- additional leave without pay
- home computer (both remote access and hardware)
- Internet access
- insurance (life and income protection)
- flexible hours (enabling working from home and flexi-days)
- car packaging (putting car-leasing payments though pre-tax)
- car parking
- paid maternity and paternity leave
- leave in lieu of pay
- additional superannuation payments
- childcare (on-site or off-site)
- discounted computer hardware and software (available through the employer's bulk discounts)
- share options
- discounts on company products.

## The Bonus

One of the major areas of negotiation could be the bonus. Many companies these days speak of OTE (On Target Earning) and KPI (Key Performance Indicators). Say, for instance, an employer offers an OTE of 200K, base 150K plus car with bonus subject to KPI.

This means the On Target Earning is $200 000. The base salary is $150 000 annually. A fully maintained company vehicle will take this to $165 000, with the remaining $35 000 to be paid as a bonus, subject to you reaching the Key Performance Indicators.

The Key Performance Indicators are generally key result areas specific to the role. They may be something tangible (like sales targets) or something more subjective (such as an assessment by a supervisor). Either way, a good company with a well-organised human resources structure will have 'scoped' the role by surveying people within the organisation to ascertain the targets. Those targets are then used as benchmarks to access the bonus.

Some companies will offer a number of the many options available in a package. Others will offer none. Generally the organisation will have a policy that is set in stone. If that policy is innovative, the company will be open to suggestions and help you to put together a package that suits your particular needs. Others will simply say they do not negotiate on packages because it will throw their entire employment structure out of kilter: what one employee gets, all employees will want. Generally speaking, if a company is open to negotiation it will be the case group-wide.

As a general rule of thumb, we find that US-headquartered companies will include more perks in packages as a matter of course than will other firms. For instance, many US firms will include full health insurance in a middle-level to senior-level employment package since medical bills are so expensive in the USA. This is a policy offered to employees at branch offices around the world.

Obviously, you won't be able to work through these conditions while sitting at the final interview. You will need financial advice and perhaps an accountant to calculate the way the package should be structured so it is most beneficial to your bottom line.

The main thing is that the overall package is within the range of what it would take to make you change your present situation. If it is, then the details can be worked out later. If the package is within your range and everything else about the position suits, it could be a case of accepting the position 'subject to an acceptable package being negotiated'.

There is, of course, more than one way to negotiate a package. You can either do it yourself, or have a third party negotiate on your behalf. If you are negotiating for yourself, there are guidelines that can make this potentially difficult endeavour relatively painless and successful. Negotiation coach Michael Chaffers offers ten tips on Monster.com for successful salary negotiations. These are equally applicable to increasing your package in an existing workplace or when trying to settle on a package with your prospective employer.

## Top Ten Tips for Successful Salary Negotiations

1. **Be persuasive.**
   It is hard to force your boss or prospective boss to increase your compensation, and trying to do so can potentially damage your working relationship. On the other hand, it is much easier to persuade the boss that it might benefit the organisation to pay you more and that doing so will likely improve the way you deal with each other as you go forward.

2. **Aim high and be realistic.**
   Many researchers have found a strong correlation between people's aspirations and the results they achieve in negotiation. At the same time, you want to suggest ideas to which your employer can realistically say yes.

3. ***Start off with the right tone.***

   To be persuasive, you want to let your employer or prospective employer know that you will listen and seek to understand his or her viewpoint. At the same time you will expect them to do the same for you, so you can work together to address this issue. Avoid ultimatums, threats or other coercive behaviour.

4. ***Clarify your interests.***

   Your compensation should satisfy a range of needs, not just salary. Make sure you have thought about other types of compensation that would be valuable as well, like profit sharing, stock options that vest immediately, a bonus, greater work responsibilities, quicker promotion schedule, increased leave or flexible hours.

5. ***Anticipate your employer's interests.***

   Just like you, your employer has needs and concerns to satisfy. To persuade them to say yes, your ideas will have to address those interests.

6. ***Create several options.***

   Joint brainstorming is the most effective way to find ideas that satisfy everyone's interests. Brainstorming works best when you separate it from commitment. First create possible solutions, then decide among them.

7. ***Focus on objective criteria.***

   It is far easier to persuade someone to agree with your proposal if it is firmly grounded on objective criteria, such as what similar firms pay people of your experience, or what others in the firm are paid.

8. ***Think through your alternatives.***

   In case you cannot persuade the employer to say yes, you need to have a Plan B to satisfy your interests. Part of preparation is creating a specific action plan so that you know what you'll do if you have to walk away from the table.

9. ***Prepare thoughtfully to achieve your goals.***
   This is the only aspect of your negotiations you can completely control. To have advantage of all the previous advice, you have to invest a significant amount of your time and energy.

10. ***Review to learn.***
    The only way you can really improve your ability to negotiate is to explicitly learn from your experiences. After you finish negotiations, reflect on what you did that worked well, and what you might want to do differently in the future.

## RECRUITMENT AGENTS

If you do not want to do the negotiating yourself, you may wish to ask a friend or associate to handle this side of the employment process. You may have an agent or business manager who will negotiate on your behalf for a set percentage. You may ask your accountant or business adviser to help you table a log of suggestions.

When people apply for a job through a recruitment firm, the negotiating process is often carried out by the recruitment agent. One of the reasons recruitment firms are so successful is that they handle the potentially uncomfortable subject of money on the client's behalf.

The recruiter will work in one of three ways:
- they will have been appointed by an organisation to find a suitable employee, or
- they will have been approached by someone who is looking for work and wants to be put in touch with possible employers, or

- they will have been appointed by a firm and introduced a suitable job seeker who is on their books (in which case they are working for both parties).

Regardless of whom the recruitment company is acting for, the bill will be paid by the employer who will pay a percentage of the successful client's first year salary. It is for this reason that recruiters will always be looking for the best package for the successful applicant, but there is more to it than pushing an applicant in the hope of scoring a large fee. The aim of the recruiter is to gain and maintain a good reputation in the market. Therefore, just as important as securing a large salary for a job seeker, is the success and longevity of the employer–employee relationship. A recruiter who earns a reputation for pushing highly paid job seekers who leave their positions after a few months will not stay in business for long.

Therefore, always go with the larger, better-known firms. They know what they are doing: their reputation depends on it and you can bet your pay on it.

## CASE STUDY
## Lawyer to Celebrity Manager and Promoter: Chris, 32

When he was at university studying law, Chris had a weekly routine that was set in stone. A sports fanatic, he would buy the magazine that covered his favourite football code and read it 'cover to cover' before returning to lectures. 'My studies had to wait until I had read every story,' he said.

With that fanaticism it is probably not surprising that working as a lawyer could not satisfy Chris and within four years of graduation he had moved in another direction – to sports management. Some six years later, he heads his own firm representing some of the best-known athletes in the world and turning over millions of dollars a year.

But, as so often is the case in successful career changes, it all started small, and from a most unlikely source. Two of Chris's best mates at high school went on to university with him. One, like him, studied law. The other, who was a promising Rugby player, studied economics.

After five years of study, Chris and his law-student friend joined firms to do their 'articles'. A two-year process, this meant working for law firms as articled clerks. The firm Chris joined was a hundred kilometres away, so he and his mate began communicating via fax. The fax messages helped the friends keep in touch and led to Chris discovering that his friend had a hidden talent as a poet.

We would write ridiculous notes to each other, things like list-ing our favourite football teams – made up entirely of players with beards, that sort of thing. I would come in on a Monday and there waiting for me was a poem he had written about something some athlete had done on the weekend. He kept writing them and they were getting better and better, so I asked him if he would mind if I tried to do something with them. He had no problems with it, so I started sending them off to newspapers and magazines.

A daily newspaper printed one of the poems, a few magazines followed and soon they were ringing Chris and commissioning his friend's poetry to mark major sporting events or milestones. Chris heard of a tribute lunch being organised in honour of a well-known sportsman and offered his friend's service – not only to write a poem, but to recite it as well. A fee was negotiated and the night was a huge success. More speaking engagements and TV appearances followed. A book of poems was a big seller and Chris negotiated a long-term TV contract. Soon the emerging celebrity gave up working as a lawyer to concentrate on his new career.

Meanwhile, Chris's other friend had started on a sporting career that would see him become recognised as one of the most talented footballers in the world. Chris offered to find him some speaking engagements as well, so when Rugby turned professional and the sport's administrators came knocking with huge offers, it was only natural that he should ask Chris to act on his behalf.

> At this stage I was working in a law firm specialising in personal injury and insurance litigation. And it was driving me crazy. I was interacting with clients, but it wasn't the sort of interaction I needed. It became pretty obvious that straight law wasn't for me. I had always thought that in a perfect world I would become a sports manager. In fact, soon after I graduated, I wrote to one of the major management companies offering my services. They never replied.

Today Chris is in direct competition with that firm and they can only look at his list of clients with envy. Of course such a stable of blue-chip clients was just a dream when Chris decided to walk away from law and go out into the world of sports management.

> The change of direction was never about money. It was about going to work every day feeling happy and looking forward to getting to the office. When I was a lawyer if I spoke to someone I had to time the conversation and bill the client. That just wasn't the way I wanted to spend the rest of my life.

Once he made the decision to follow this new career path, Chris was approached by the owner of a small but successful sports management agency. The owner offered Chris a twenty-five per cent stake in the company in return for bringing his two clients and helping expand the business. While Chris had offers from other organisations, he saw joining this firm as part of a learning curve.

I did my research and learnt that the edge this company had was that it was marketing oriented. I knew that I could handle the contract side of things. With my legal background I had experience in negotiating, but the side of the business that is more important is in developing an income stream for your clients outside the contract. That is what I had to learn about.

The business just snowballed. From one of my clients I would be introduced to another, who would introduce me to two more. Then my business partner decided he wanted to go back to his first love, which was music, and I bought the rest of the business.

Chris now employs six full-time staff and has fifteen high-profile clients who earn millions. It is a successful company in a highly competitive field, but Chris says the bottom line is still the enjoyment level.

I feel fulfilled beyond my wildest dreams. To me the satisfaction is in getting the best out of people. I like the feeling of helping people on a journey. You are helping them set goals and then achieve them, both financial and personal. It can be very satisfying. There are some downsides. Some people can expect a lot and giving them the time they would like gets harder the older you get and the more family commitments you have of your own. But any downside is more than compensated for by the benefits of the job.

While Chris describes what he does as 'definitely a dream career' he says it is still a springboard rather than a final destination.

The work I do naturally leads to other areas. Through working with the athletes I see how events are run and think of ways to run them better, so we are now running some events of our own. I honestly believe that sport is a very precious commodity. It has to run the right way and be protected.

We also come into contact with the sponsors who finance the major sporting organisations and that is an area I would like to explore – working on their behalf to see they get the best value for their money.

The way that sport interacts with pay television and other forms of broadcasting is an area which is changing so rapidly that it opens up enormous possibilities. I find that all very exciting. It will take people like me in directions we can't even imagine. It is definitely an ongoing process and I am enjoying the journey every inch of the way.

# 10

# saying goodbye

Achieving your dream career is an ongoing process. As in all things, whether a personal relationship, sport or work, the goals you set for yourself are constantly changing. Once you have reached one goal, you will want to set another and go for it. In terms of your dream career this may mean in order to achieve it you may have to leave where you are working and go elsewhere. Your career path might be blocked or the organisation you work for may not offer the opportunity you desire.

The thing to remember is that no one gets where they want to be immediately. Your first job might be a good starting point, but to see it as a final destination is both short-sighted and defeatist. You can never climb a ladder by staying frozen on the first rung.

## LEAVING WITH GRACE AND DIGNITY

While moving from organisation to organisation might be an accepted part of working life, the way you leave is of vital importance. Always remember, when leaving a job you are not saying 'goodbye', you are saying 'see you later'. You cannot predict the future and there is every chance that the people you are leaving will be your workmates again before your journey is completed. You may return to the company – or the company might just return to you.

One of the best-known stories in our industry concerns the man who left a company and joined its competitor. There is nothing wrong with that, it happens all the time, but what this man did was wrong. Before leaving, he 'rolled a few hand grenades' through the office. In effect, he told his superiors that he did not like or respect them or the way they did business, and told his former workmates what a lame lot of no-hopers he considered them to be. Within a year the company he had moved to took over the company he had left and he was asked to work with his former colleagues – almost in the same job he had held previously. Needless to say, the atmosphere was somewhat strained. The former employers were not happy to be working with this man and it took a lot of negotiation on both sides before the situation could be resolved. He got fired.

This sort of thing happens all the time. Companies are bought and merged; industries are restructured and shrink. The options of where to work and with whom become smaller virtually overnight. One never knows who will be in the office next door next month.

Just as company buy-outs or mergers might place you, through no conscious choice of your own, back with the company where you started, the situation might arise where you want to go back to your former employer almost immediately. One of the main reasons people decide to leave a job is because their career path is being blocked by someone who has no intention of leaving. Just as you read of footballers leaving a club because one of the best players in the world is holding down the position they covet, so too do employees leave an organisation they love because the person ahead of them looks like staying put for decades. Invariably, as soon as they leave the company and start a new job, that person will, for one reason or another, suddenly depart and getting the dream job becomes a possibility. It might be six months or it might be six weeks after leaving, but suddenly you are going to want that organisation to take you back.

For this reason you should look at your career as one life-long relationship. The offices and company names might change, but the people do not. In this context, just like in any relationship, it is important to give and take. Be flexible and, above all, do not slam any doors or burn any bridges.

When you leave an organisation it is a good policy to write a note of farewell to the appropriate people. If someone has been a particular supporter or mentor, thank them for their help. Let them know how much you have appreciated their support, friendship or guidance and tell them you hope to work with them again in the future. Such a letter should be succinct and sincere. Do not write to someone with whom you have not had a close relationship. Do not write in the hope of impressing someone in authority. Insincerity will only backfire and work against you. Do it for one reason only: because you mean it.

Remember, when you leave, nothing is more important than maintaining your credibility. And nothing is harder to overcome than a bad final impression. For just as first impressions are important when applying for, or starting, a new job, last impressions are equally important when you leave. For this reason you should try to leave with dignity and style. Put the organisation in front of your own circumstances and you will be remembered as someone who left because 'the timing was not right' rather than someone who was 'not the right type'.

The best way to leave a company is with the chief executive shaking your hand and saying, in all sincerity: 'It has been a pleasure working with you. We would welcome you back at any time.'

## OBTAINING A STRONG REFERENCE

When you leave a job there is one thing you should leave behind – a good impression – and there is one thing you should take with you – a good reference.

The best reference is not necessarily the most glowing. It is the most truthful. Rest assured, if you have reached the stage in the employment process where a recruiter, consultant or prospective employer is in possession of your references, they will check them. And if the referee is being evasive or less than open in certain areas, it will stand out like a beacon.

The same if the referee you have chosen is inappropriate. Remember, when it comes to hiring someone the most important thing is not whether they know their stuff, it is whether they can be successful and productive in the new environment.

For this reason, it is not always appropriate for your referee to be the highest executive in an organisation. An experienced recruiter will know just by looking at your previous position whether the chief executive will have come in contact with you and your work on a daily basis. The recruiter will be far more interested in the views of your immediate supervisor. In the business of executive employment, everyone knows the story of the salesman who received a glowing reference from the chairman of the company, got the job – and was a disaster. When the new employer mentioned this to the man's previous marketing director he was not surprised. 'Why didn't you ask me?' he said. 'I could have told you that guy wouldn't have fitted in over there.' Why indeed?

For this reason, when asking for a reference do not aim too far away. These days an environmental check is seen as far more important than a skills check. A recruiter does not just want to know whether you can do the job. They want to know whether you can do the job in the new environment.

In requesting a reference it is therefore appropriate that you guide the referee. Let them know what you would like them to comment on. For instance, you might say: 'As you know I am leaving and I would appreciate it if you could write a few words about how I did my work and how I fitted into the organisation.'

Remember, the majority of people who fail in an organisation fail not because they can't do the job, but because they can't do it in a particular environment. For this reason, your reference is very important. It should let the prospective employer know exactly the type of person you are. The employer doesn't want to hire someone who will not fit in, any more than you want to go to a work environment where you will not feel comfortable.

As in any successful relationship, both sides have to feel they have made the right choice.

**CASE STUDY**
**Journalist to Public Relations Consultant:**
**Steve, 48**

When Steve left school he started as a copy boy at one of the major metropolitan daily newspapers.

I made tea, collected mail from the airport, monitored the police radio to see if there was anything the reporters should be covering and ran copy (taking the reporters' stories typed on paper to the editors). After about a year I applied for a cadetship with the largest suburban newspaper chain in Australia and was successful. Thanks to the year's experience I had with the city newspaper I had to do only three years of the four-year cadetship. After six months I was a C-grade journalist, a year later I was upgraded to a B-grade. A year later I was an A-grade and, at the age of 22 I was appointed editor of a suburban newspaper.

Steve admits his rise up the ranks was too quick and after a year he was replaced as editor of the paper and given a job back at head office, where all the papers in the chain were printed. It was there that he found his true niche, as a production editor, overseeing the editing and printing process for all papers in the group. After a few years he was given another opportunity to edit a paper and this time, thanks to his greater maturity and experience, it proved a much more successful posting.

After a few years I was headhunted by one of the major metropolitan papers. I had eighteen months as features editor and then, when I turned down the role of night editor for the second time, I moved to another daily paper in the group as features editor.

Steve's refusal to take the full-time night shift – a role which would have assured him of a steady rise up the ranks in the paper – was one of several clashes he had with the hierarchy as he bucked the system.

I was a very good production man who liked to be left alone to do my job. I was good at producing a section of the paper, but no good at sitting in editorial meetings or playing the corporate game. When I went to a planning meeting, I would show the editor what I was going to have in the paper the next day, not sit around and discuss. It came to a head when the editor came back from a meeting with the chief executive and said to me: 'I was just asked by the boss of this company what would be on the feature page of this newspaper tomorrow and I couldn't tell him because you never tell me what you are doing.' I think it just became obvious to everyone that I wasn't willing to become part of the system.

I stayed for a few more years, but finally I couldn't take it any more. I had always been allowed a high level of autonomy. I was an action man. If the deadline for the page was 6 p.m., I wanted to have it out at 4 p.m. I just wanted to run my own race. Plus the corporate game was driving me crazy. I felt people were getting promoted above their ability because they were good at playing the game. I just didn't want to be part of it any more.

Steve saw an advertisement in the newspaper calling for a journalist to join a leading public relations firm.

I didn't know how to write a resumé, so I just sat down at one of the paper's old computers and wrote my life story as if I was writing an article for a paper. I had an interview, the owner of the company asked me how much money I earned, he told me how much more he would pay me, and drew up a contract.

I started work with him, learnt how to keep count of billable hours, went to more meetings than I ever had as a journalist and hated every minute of it.

But while Steve did not fit the stereotypical picture of the silver-tongued public relations executive, his offhand approach proved to be attractive to the firm's customers.

I told one of the firm's major clients that I didn't fit the job and that I was planning to return to newspapers. He said if

I left and started my own firm he would pay me a $30 000 retainer to do his publicity. I told him that wasn't ethical, but he told me he was going to take his business elsewhere anyway, so that's what I did. One year to the day after I had joined the firm I started on my own, with that one client underwriting the start-up of the business.

Another consultant joined Steve, bringing her one client with her.

We had two staff and two clients but it just grew from there. I had great newspaper contacts, but was lousy at meetings. My partner had no newspaper experience, but she was great at presentations. It just clicked. We could give the male–female pitch.

The big thing I had was the newspaper contacts. My friends were running most of the suburban newspapers in the city and when I rang up my old contacts from the city news-papers I think they thought I still worked there. I could go along to prospective clients and say to them 'I'll write a story about you and put it in such-and-such a paper on this day.' I could virtually guarantee them a left or right page. If they didn't believe that I could do it, I'd tell them I wouldn't bill them if I didn't.

Some twenty years later, Steve's partner has moved on, but his business still flourishes. He owns his own building in a prime city location and has more business than he can handle. He says the skills he learnt as a newspaperman are still what set him apart from his competitors.

Mine is a words-driven operation. We are part of the public relations industry, but not a public relations firm. I suppose we offer a niche service. I contract a number of freelance journalists to write for me and using those same production skills I learnt when I was twenty-two years old, I produce publications for my clients. We put out trade magazines, corporate newspapers, even write and lay out advertorial pages for major newspapers, so all they have to do is push the button on the printing press.

To me and the people who work with me, it is just bread-and-butter journalism, but we have found a market. There are any number of people who can design a publication, but not many who can write.

Over the past two decades, Steve's two-person, two-client operation has evolved into a lucrative business, but he says making money was never the motivation for his change of direction.

I didn't know anything about money at first. I'd always had a job, someone always paid me so I was confident that I would always be able to make a living. What I was interested in was finding a place where I could choose the way I worked, when I worked and how I worked. By going out on my own I was able to mould a business around my needs and skills and avoid doing things that I either wasn't good at or which upset me. The more I was able to build on my strengths, the more the money came and it goes without saying that I was happier.

The funny thing was, when I went for the job at the large PR firm, they gave me a psychological test. I had to answer all these questions and at the end of it they said I had all the right answers, but that I had got to them the wrong way. They said they'd never seen a test answered like that before. The conclusion they came to was that I was a leader, but that I had difficulty taking direction from people I didn't respect. They were spot on, weren't they?

# 11

# out, but not down

Some people decide to make a career change only after long and careful consideration. They talk to their family and friends, mentors and workmates. They agonise, anguish and finally take the first, tentative steps in a different direction. Others have no choice at all. They are called into an office, rung on a telephone, maybe even e-mailed or faxed. The words are blunt and uncompromising: they have been let go. It may be termed retrenchment, downsizing or layoff. Sometimes it might even be the word 'fired'. Regardless of the form the dismissal takes, the end result is the same: they are out of a job.

Once upon a time this would have been a time for recrimination and shame. In the past, executives have been known to dress in their best suit, pack their lunch in a briefcase and head out of the house at the same time as usual – and then go and watch a movie or sit in a park until the end of the working day – anything, just so long as the neighbours or even the family weren't alerted to the humiliation. Happily those days are gone. Being retrenched is still an initially shocking and life-changing upheaval, but the stigma once attached to being out of work has largely passed.

## JOB TENURE AND CHANGE IN THE CORPORATE WORLD

Today a change of job is seen as an unavoidable by-product of changes in the commercial environment, rather than a reflection of the capabilities of the person involved. The composition of corporations is changing. They are downsizing, reorganising, merging with competitors, moving parts of their operations offshore and closing or selling off unprofitable divisions. And consequently people are losing their jobs.

The term 'downsizing' was never heard until the 1980s when corporations in the USA began, for the first time, to realise that big wasn't necessarily beautiful. When Jack Welch took over as chairman in 1981, General Electric was the tenth biggest corporation in the USA in terms of size and market capitalisation. For years the company had been growing bigger and bigger, struggling in some of its markets, holding its own and dominating in others. But that, at the time, was what big business was all about. Your profitable divisions carried your weaker ones. There was plenty of money to go around. Jack Welch disagreed. He instigated a policy of 'Number 1 or 2 – fix, sell or close.' Basically, this meant if a GE division was not the market leader or number two, it would either reach that place or be sold or closed. While such a policy would be seen as commonplace today, twenty years ago it was seen as revolutionary (visionary to some, madness to others – and shattering to those who lost their jobs in the process). Within two years GE had sold seventy-one businesses. The air-conditioning division alone had three plants and 2300 employees, but with a market share of only ten per cent, Welch, who earned the nickname 'Neutron Jack' (he got rid of all the people, but left the buildings standing) felt it had to go. This sale struck at the heart of long-time GE employees, who considered it one of the corporation's traditional divisions. However, it was small time in relation to the big picture. Between the end of 1980 (when employment was at its peak at GE) and the end of 1985, GE went from 411 000 employees to 299 000. Of the 80 000 people who had to leave the payroll, over 30 000 were in businesses the corporation sold off and about 112 000 (or nearly one in five of the total original staff) were laid off for productivity reasons.

At the same time GE was laying off staff and closing divisions, another US corporate giant, IBM ('Big Blue'), launched an advertising campaign with the slogan: 'Jobs may come and go. But people shouldn't.' That was in 1985 and IBM's promise of a 'job for life' was as well known as its blue trademark. It was a promise that IBM could not keep as 'Big Blue' emerged as a major casualty of the IT revolution. The company that had led the world in the production of mainframe computers was left behind as the microchip took over. Today IBM is another example of a company that had to downsize and reinvent itself in order to survive. It changed its role to put more emphasis on consulting, and thousands of workers had to make a major change in their working lives as a result.

It is happening all over the world. Australians only have to look at the shining Automatic Teller Machine in the wall where their local bank branch once stood to see downsizing in action. Hundreds of branches have gone and thousands of former bank workers have been forced back onto the market. The world of finance is just one industry sector that has changed dramatically over the past decade. Many people who were seduced by the short-lived dot com explosion have had to find new employment and the newspapers have been full of headlines about the collapse of major employers such as One.Tel, HIH and Ansett.

But nothing in recent times has affected employment internationally more than the 11 September 2001 terrorist attacks on the USA. In Australia since 1988 the average number of workers retrenched or laid off annually has been around 270 000 to 300 000. In the year following the 11 September terrorist attacks, the number was expected to be around 320 000. In the USA in the twelve months up to 11 September, the number of workers re-entering the market after having lost their jobs was around 200 000. Between 11 September and 31 December 2001 the number was expected to reach two million with major losses in tourism-related industries such as airlines, travel, hotels, restaurants and associated retail.

Of course the effects of 11 September on employment are unusual in the extreme. It is to be hoped that they will prove temporary and reversible. In the meantime, those people who find themselves back in the employment market will have to look for work as they did in the past, treating the process as a job in itself.

## LOSING YOUR JOB

Generally speaking, society is able to adjust to change. We accept and enjoy its benefits and see the inconveniences and disruptions associated with it as unavoidable and, in the long term, inconsequential. That is, of course, until we lose our job. When that happens, in that first stunning moment we go through the full gamut of negative emotions: shock, disbelief, anger, upset. A scene in the film *Broadcast News* captures the feeling in an amusing, insightful way. The television program around which the movie is based is given the chop. As one long-time employee, who has just been called into the boss's office to be told the bad news, is leaving, the boss puts his arm around him and says, 'Bill, I'm really sorry. Is there anything I can do?' 'Well,' says Bill calmly, 'I'd be really happy if you would die soon.'

When we are told that our cosy cocoon has been torn away and we are back in the cold, forbidding world, recrimination is an obvious emotion. This is particularly so when the loss of the job has come after a power struggle. The person who is being shown the door feels they have not only lost a job, they have lost a battle. No matter how the end comes, whether out of the blue or at the end of a long process, it always seems sudden and the prospects appear bleak. Depression often sets in.

## REGAINING EMPLOYMENT

The good news is that this feeling is perfectly normal but, in most cases, an over-reaction. Of the 320 000 people who lost their jobs in Australia in the year following 11 September 2001, most will be re-employed – and sooner rather than later. A recent survey showed that the average time spent between jobs for people:

- aged under 45 in jobs earning less than $50 000 was 7 weeks for women and 11 weeks for men
- aged over 50 in jobs earning over $50 000 was 14 weeks for women and 17 for men.

Why the difference in the genders? Women in a retrenchment situation are less ego-driven, more flexible and more adaptable. They are more willing to give another industry or profession a try, whereas male pride pushes a man to try to achieve a better job in the same industry, so he can prove to his old employers that he is not only doing well, but he is doing better. Often, in fact, this is the case. People can find a better job in their old industry, but at the same time, they should be open to change. Now, more than ever before, there are more options available, and more help provided to explore them.

## OUTPLACEMENT

Since the early 1990s many Australian corporations have provided retrenched employees with access to outplacement – a range of services aimed at helping them get over their dismissal and back into the work force. The low unemployment rate and strong demand for quality workers in the USA in recent years has meant there has been little need for companies to spend the $1500 to $2500 (AU$3000 to $5000) it costs for employees to go through the outplacement process. The fallout from the recent traumatic events in the States has changed this, with outplacement now a major part of HR policy in many US corporations.

In its earliest form, outplacement was targeted primarily at helping clients overcome the psychological shock of losing their job. When downsizing and retrenchment were relatively new phenomena, cases of dismissed executives being found in a foetal position on the boardroom floor were not uncommon! Outplacement in the early 1990s consisted mainly of psychological counselling to help overcome shock, anger and depression.

Nowadays, just as the public perception of being laid off has changed, so has the nature of outplacement. Once a psychological process, it is now more a physical aid to finding and securing a new job. This process takes the form of coaching in such activities as preparing effective resumés and perfecting interview techniques, plus giving access to any number of services to help target the most suitable future career path. A company can offer outplacement support by granting access to the office and its computer, secretarial and Internet facilities, right up to hiring the services of a professional outplacement specialist who will offer counselling and advice on how to access the relevant online information (such as resumé and interview simulators), and help with researching desirable industries and prospective employers. The company will pinpoint suitable career opportunities and arrange interviews. In some cases, the outplacement specialist's most important function might just be to provide a much-needed sounding-board. Sometimes outplacement will result in a quick return to the workplace, maybe even in the same industry in virtually the same position the worker has just left; other times it will be the first step towards a different outlook, realising untapped potential and exploring a new career path.

## The opportunity to adjust your focus

Many retrenched people have been working for the one company or in the same industry for many years. In that time the whole nature of employment and the workplace environment has changed enormously. For people who have been in a virtual employment time-warp, outplacement is the start of looking at employment in a radically new way. Some fifteen or twenty years ago work was all-encompassing, the undisputed major part of an employee's life. The saying 'I work to live, not live to work' had not been coined and in many cases people found themselves a job and tailored their life to fit in with it. Now it is the other way around. Outplacement counselling will often motivate the retrenched worker to re-evaluate their priorities before deciding which career path to follow. The ideal is to achieve a more balanced approach, with the perfect job one that fits the employee's desired lifestyle and personal aspirations.

## Your entitlements

Workers in Australia are morally, if not legally, entitled to outplacement services and, if they are not offered by the employer, they should be requested. The majority of corporations offer outplacement as a matter of policy and companies would find it difficult to refuse on legal grounds if challenged.

But even before dismissed workers avail themselves of whatever outplacement services are available, they should explore certain options. The first is to ensure they have no way of staying with the company, if they feel that is their preferred option. In many cases dismissals are forced upon employers for economic reasons. It may be the case that a compromise would suit both parties. The worker may prefer to work fewer days or shorter hours and take a cut in salary and the employer may find that this is a solution to their problems as well.

If no compromise is possible, the dismissed worker must ensure they receive all their entitlements. These will depend on the way they have been dismissed.

## Three Main Causes for Dismissal

1. Misconduct
2. Poor performance
3. Redundancy.

If a worker has been made redundant, the employer is not able to replace them. Needless to say, there are many grey areas when it comes to dismissal. The reasons that someone is asked to leave a company are often open to interpretation. Who sets the parameters for 'poor performance' and when is 'redefining' a dismissed worker's role and offering it to someone else really 'replacement'? For this reason dismissed employees should always seek professional advice if they feel they have been treated unfairly – and even more importantly, the terms and conditions of a job should be carefully laid out in a contract in the first instance to reduce the chances of dispute. As film producer Sam Goldwyn said: 'A verbal contract isn't worth the paper it's written on.' If you dispute your dismissal, your lawyer will be powerless unless the conditions were written down and signed by both parties before you took up employment. Specialist employment lawyers are available to help in such cases, as well as making sure you receive your entitlement in terms of promised stock options and payouts. They will also determine whether you are, in fact, redundant or have been unfairly dismissed.

While an employment lawyer may be needed to ensure you receive all your entitlements, a financial advisor will help you to decide the best way to spend them. Obviously it will depend on the amount of money you receive, and your personal situation in terms of financial commitments, but there are tax-effective ways to disperse lump-sum payments, and these should all be explored. Such financial advice is often provided as part of the outplacement service. It can also be provided free of charge, along with legal advice, as a benefit of trade union membership.

The amount of money you receive will, of course, depend on a number of factors: the most important being seniority and length of service. While senior management positions are complicated because of the number of perks (such as stock options) included in contracts, the vast majority of redundancy payments will come under the generally accepted formula of two to three weeks' pay for each year of service, plus accrued holiday and sick pay. This will differ from industry to industry, depending on individual company policy and award requirements set through union arbitration. In the UK and some European countries redundancy payments are made by the Government as part of the social security arrangements.

## MOVING ON

It is always advisable to leave on good terms, no matter how the parting of the ways occurred. Remember, even though you might only barely contain your rage at the time of dismissal, you are going to need that person who is currently showing you the door to put in a good word to your future employers – and final impressions can be lasting. Letters of recommendation from employers (similar to Sam Goldwyn's verbal contracts) aren't worth a great deal on their own. When it comes to the crunch, prospective employers or recruitment firms will require verbal references. Letters of recommendation from clients, on the other hand, can be very handy. Experienced recruiters will know that someone leaving a company should be able to find at least one former superior to write something nice. A reference from a client will carry more weight.

While it is advisable to start the re-employment process as soon as possible, it is also imperative that you do not start too soon. It is our experience that dismissed employees should take a ten-day break before throwing themselves full-time into the job of securing work. By all means have one or two initial meetings with an outplacement specialist, settle your misgivings and check out what services are available, but then get out of town. Whether you realise it or not, when you have been retrenched or dismissed, you have been psychologically wounded. You feel hurt and angry, your pride has been dented and you are worried for your future. To start searching for work in that frame of mind is counter-productive. Even if you do not realise it, you are radiating the wrong signal. You will have to sell yourself to a new employer and any emotional baggage will be immediately evident to an experienced interviewer. People do not want to hire employees who are bitter and twisted. They certainly won't feel well disposed towards someone who wastes their valuable interviewing time ranting and raving about the perceived treachery of their previous employer. Take the ten days, get away and get healthy. It will be hard at first, the first three days of your break you will be preoccupied with the injustice of what has happened in the past and the uncertainty of what is going to happen in the future. By day four and five you will start to see things in a different light. By day seven and eight you will be refreshed. By nine and ten, you will have regained a positive attitude and feel ready to take on the world.

The best way to launch your attack on the job market is as close at hand as the nearest computer keyboard. There are literally thousands of pages of information covering all aspects of the recruitment process on the Internet. TMP's online career portal Monster.com has an enormous database covering just about any eventuality, from targeting resumés to virtual interviews. There are also numerous articles written by experts in the field, such as this one by American writer Paul W. Barada.

One of the more frequently asked questions is 'How do I explain getting fired to a prospective employer?' While there isn't an easy answer to this question, there are two important steps you can take to minimise the potentially negative effects of being terminated, separated or whatever euphemism you want to substitute for the word 'fired'.

First, be honest. There is no good way to sugarcoat being fired, so the best course of action is to honestly tell a prospective employer, as objectively and candidly as possible, your view of what happened. The worst thing any job seeker can do is to be less than honest about the reason for leaving an employer and then have somebody check your references and discover you lied. That's a sure ticket to the unemployment office. Part of the difficulty in giving a simple answer comes from the multitude of reasons why people get fired. There is no stock phrase that fits every situation when it comes to explaining to a prospective employer why you left your last job. The only certain advice is, don't lie about it! Being objective and not placing blame are key. Not every job is perfect for every employee, and no one can get along with everybody all the time. Sometimes personalities clash. Sometimes the realities of the job don't match the expectations. The list goes on and on, but more often than not, firings either involve personalities, performance or both. It is essential for the person who was fired to realise that the circumstances that led to it, more often than not, involved at least two points of view. That's where being objective comes into play.

Every person who has been fired should take the time to calmly evaluate what actually happened and what his or her role in it truly was. In other words, it probably wouldn't be a good idea to tell a prospective employer, 'It was all their fault. I was a perfect employee every day, and I was an outstanding performer in every aspect of my job. They were totally wrong to fire me!' Even if that were true, who would believe it? Remember the old adages: 'It takes two people to have an argument' and 'Nobody's perfect'. To minimise the potential damage of being fired, be prepared to explain how you've gained wisdom about yourself and your abilities from the experience.

Once you've had time to take a good long look in the mirror, start thinking about what you could have done differently that might have led to another result and what you'll do differently in the future. If, for instance, it was a matter of a personality clash, be prepared to talk about it in the first-person plural. '*We* just couldn't work together.' That's how you let a prospective employer know you have critically evaluated both sides of the situation. Then use that as a springboard to highlight the positives that came from the experience. It's critical to take some blame. You might say, 'I didn't have a clear understanding of their expectations' as opposed to 'They didn't tell me what their expectations were'. Nearly everyone can improve in some area, and that's what you want to stress to a prospective employer.

Getting fired isn't the sin, not learning anything from it is. So, the best advice is to be honest about what happened and explain what you learned from the experience. If you follow that, you'll find most prospective employers will be favourably impressed with you.

While such information is invaluable when the time comes to actually start interviewing for jobs, initially, one of the best things about outplacement is that you will have somewhere to go. To make the most of outplacement, it is important that the prospective employee treats finding a job as their new job – a job they put as much into, maybe even more, than they have given to paid employment in the past! Everyone approaches finding a new job differently. Some feel a few hours a day is enough, others will give it a forty-hour week. They will arrive at the outplacement centre as if they were arriving at their office and follow their day plan with the attention to detail of a military operation. They will prepare resumés, practise their interviewing technique, scan the newspaper ads, log their resumés online, check jobs available on Internet employment services, network old contacts, research companies and industries, and follow up cover letters and interviews.

Some people will also embark on some form of retraining,

although this is less common. Most likely retraining will take the form of updating or upscaling previously held qualifications in order to meet industry standards. We find that about 10 per cent of people who are forced to look for a new job will make a complete change of direction. They may find a different job in a different industry or market, but they will still be using the skills they honed in their previous employment.

Where applicable we advise the job seeker to make a day plan which includes setting aside time to spend with their spouse, children or partner. Searching for work can also be a very positive time to catch up on some of the more pleasant pursuits that you would not normally have the time to do. Pick your kids up from school, go for a walk along the beach with your partner. Go fishing or play golf. Read that novel. After all, you won't have as much time to do those things when you get a job. And, despite what you might have thought the day you got called into the office to receive that chilling news, you will get another job. Not only another job, but most likely a better one. It is our experience that 98 per cent of people who go through our outplacement program move on to a more enjoyable position that suits them better and is more desirable in some way. Inevitably they tell us that being forced to move was the catalyst for better things. Nobody likes change, but, in retrospect, it is often the best thing that could have happened.

## CASE STUDY
### From Typesetter to Sales Representative: Joe, 56

Right through his working life, Joe had been involved in the printing industry. He started as a typesetter and, as technology overtook that role, he became a graphic designer. At the age of 55, Joe's life was turned upside down when his company downsized and he was retrenched.

He was naturally upset, but cautiously optimistic that he could pursue a new career to end his working days. Joe was referred to an outplacement specialist and threw himself into the task of finding a new career path.

> I suppose it helped that I was very open to change. I embraced all the workshops and followed all the advice on things like writing effective resumés and covering letters. It wasn't easy because I was applying for all kinds of roles way outside what I had done before and, at my age, people weren't willing to take a punt on me. It started to become pretty frustrating when I couldn't even get in the door for interviews. I suppose I could have given up then, but I persisted and one of the online programs the outsourcing firm offered showed I was particularly suited to sales.

Working with the outplacement specialists, Joe narrowed his search down to landing a sales role, with a short-term and long-term goal. Short-term, his goal was a casual sales role with a national retail outlet. Long-term, he hoped to gain enough experience to be able to move to other companies.

It then took Joe eight weeks to get a casual role with one of Australia's largest and most respected retail organisations and within six weeks this was upgraded to a permanent position. In the future, with experience under his belt Joe will be able to apply for more senior roles within this company or move to others that are seeking a solid sales background.

> All up I was out of work for five months from the beginning of the process until I got my first casual job. It was pretty frustrating at times, but now I can look back at it as a learning experience. If I hadn't been retrenched and done that online

program, I would never have discovered the role that I am best suited for. The way I have settled into my job and picked it up makes me realise that I have always had a natural aptitude for sales, even though I had never worked in that area. Because I am doing something I am suited for, I find that I pick things up pretty easily and because of that I am really enjoying my new career. I like dealing with people and advising on what product is best for them and I suppose there is also the satisfaction that comes from embarking on a new career path at a time when many people think their working lives are nearly over. It makes me feel proud and invigorated. I'm like a kid again starting out on my first job!

# 12

# starting over

When you start a new job you should be yourself – after all, if all has happened as it should, the person your new employer has hired should be the person you really are. In other words, you shouldn't have to play a role when you go to work. As we have said before, the most successful people are those whose work personality is no different to their personality away from the workplace. When you have found a career path that is closely aligned to your outside interests and talents, you will be on the path to success.

It all begins at the interview, where your future employer gets the first glimpse of your personality. If you have to lie to get the job, chances are it is not going to work out for either of you. It might be a cliché, but when it comes to interviews, honesty is the best policy. No doubt you will be asked a question such as: 'What are your weaknesses?' The interviewer will have far more respect for a high degree of self-analysis than for clichés. If you answer the question with 'I work too hard' or 'I am such a perfectionist that those around me can't keep up', it is likely that the interviewer will be turned off immediately. Don't be afraid to take a good, hard look at yourself and your performance. The fact is that everyone has weaknesses. The key is identifying your weaknesses so that you can work on overcoming them. Therefore, when you are asked to list your weaknesses, go ahead and list them: 'I have a bad temper sometimes', 'I tend to have problems delegating' or 'I have to work on prioritising'. You will be amazed at how intuitive interviewers can be. If you show that you have taken stock of your life and isolated any weaknesses, it will be perceived as a positive, rather than a negative.

If not, and you somehow get through the interview process based on a lie, it will eventually come crashing down around you. A person can maintain a masquerade for only so long and when things are at their toughest is when you will be judged. One's inherent personality does not change. Under pressure people will always revert to type.

## MAKING A GOOD IMPRESSION

We heard recently of an Australian salesman with excellent credentials who, due to family commitments, relocated to an organisation in New Zealand. His new employer was delighted to have him on board and looked forward to making the most of his experience. The first day the employee turned up for work his new boss called the entire sales staff into the conference room. 'This is Bill,' he said. 'He is a real hot-shot who has done some sensational things in Australia. I haven't been happy with the performance of some of you in recent months and I want you all to watch the way Bill works and learn from him.'

As Bill told us later: 'It was hardly the perfect start. By the time the boss walked out of the conference room everyone in the company hated me.'

While Bill is an extreme example it is hardly unusual. Employees are always a bit threatened when someone new enters their domain. They naturally wonder how this newcomer's presence will affect them and the niche they have carved for themselves in the company. Without words to the effect even being uttered, they think: 'If the boss has seen fit to hire this person, they must be dissatisfied with the way things have been going. My future must be in jeopardy.' Of course, in some cases this is true, but in others it is simply a case of the employer feeling the newcomer will enhance what is already a winning team. Either way, as the new kid on the block, it is best to employ a softly-softly approach when starting a new job.

## Undersell and Over-deliver

This is the key to making a good impression in your new workplace.

As Bill's example shows, there are two distinct levels of people a newcomer must both work with and impress: the boss and the peers. The way to get along with both parties is to perform above expectations. For this reason it is best not to make wild claims or boast of previous achievements. If this happens, workmates will be not only be watching for you to fail, they will be hoping for it. No one likes arrogance, especially from someone who is new and has not had a chance to demonstrate their more endearing side. Raising the expectations of your superiors to unobtainable heights is just as foolhardy. By all means, set high goals for yourself, but keep them quiet. Let your actions speak louder than words. Remember, the ideal employee is the one who does a good job – and gets along with their workmates while doing it.

Most people know the old adage: 'Be nice to people on your way up, because you are bound to meet them on your way down.'

We prefer: 'Be nice to people on your way up, or they won't want to work for you when you get to the top.' It is true. If you aspire to a level of leadership in any organisation, you are in fact hoping to become captain of a team, and a team is only as strong as the cohesion of the individual members. The first thing a leader does is to try to get the team working together, pulling in the one direction. It will be a lot easier to achieve if you have earned the respect of your co-workers as you worked your way up the ladder.

## MOTIVATION

Everyone is responsible for motivating themselves. It is not up to the organisation or your boss to do it for you. To rely on your employers to get you going each day is a cop-out. Nevertheless everyone has a different level of motivation. Some people are naturally self-motivated, some are adept at setting goals and others need a daily rev-up. The key is to find what it is that motivates you, and use it to maximum effect. Top-level athletes are invariably experts at self-motivation. Australian cricketer Ian Healy kept a log of his feelings at different times in his career. After his greatest successes, Healy would immediately write a list of the feelings he had leading up to that success, the aim being to re-create the winning atmosphere in a virtual 'success incubator'. What Healy was doing, was expelling negatives from his personal space, and allowing only positive vibes to get through. Likewise US sprint queen Marion Jones, who soon after being beaten in the 100 metres at the 2001 World Championships (her first loss over the distance in four years) admitted that the loss had thrown her. 'It had been so long since I was beaten that I wasn't sure which emotions were applicable,' she said. Now that's a winning attitude. So confident was she of success, that her subconscious wasn't equipped to cope with a loss.

Similar to the athlete who surrounds themself with winning

'triggers', workers must ensure that they are employed in an atmosphere that spurs them on. If you are someone who needs to be motivated by those around you, look for a team role in a structured company. Self-starters should work for themselves. There are those who prefer to work in the background, while others deal with customers. Whatever the case, it is no good thinking that an unsatisfactory work environment will work out. You must take the initiative. If you are not working in a position or industry that gets your emotional and creative juices flowing, move. It's as simple as that. Get out and find a position that does.

Of course the greatest motivation that anyone can have is working towards a goal, which makes it all the more surprising to realise that very few people have clearly defined work goals. They work to earn enough money to pay the bills, and while that is a worthy ambition, it is hardly an inspirational one.

What is the perfect work goal? The one that is most closely aligned to one's life goals. For instance, early in your working life you might have the aim to save enough money to buy a stereo system; a few years later it might be to be able to afford an overseas holiday or a new car. The specifics of the goal aren't what is important for motivation, having the emotional commitment to a goal is. If working harder leads to a greater reward that in turn makes you a happier, more contented individual, you have all the motivation you'll ever need.

## PROMOTION

In an ideal world, it works like this: you do your job well, the boss notices you and you are promoted. Needless to say, it isn't a perfect world and it doesn't always happen that way. Any number of factors can determine whether you are promoted. Regardless of whether you are involved in what is broadly termed 'office politics' or not, 'politics' for want of a better word, will play a major part in your progress throughout a firm and, indeed, throughout a career. How many times have you heard someone bemoan the fact that a co-worker has received the break they were hoping for with the explanation: 'It's just politics – the boss likes him more than he likes me.' No doubt if you are working in a large organisation, you will have heard it often. Of course the boss is going to promote the person he or she likes more – if that favouritism comes from the fact that the person does a particularly good job.

There are two kinds of office politics: overt and covert. Being overtly political would consist of taking your boss to lunch, finding where he or she plays golf and making sure you are there when they are looking for an extra player to make up a foursome. Some people will play the political game and it might even work – for a while. But as we said earlier in this chapter, a masquerade will last only so long. Successful companies do not operate on personalities, they live or die on results. Overt politics might open a door, but unless the politicking is backed by serious ability, sooner or later – usually sooner – that door will slam.

On the other hand, working hard, taking on any assignment offered and doing it well, will eventually earn just as much attention as a bottle of Scotch or a bunch of flowers at Christmas time. In its own way, doing a good job is covertly political. It will get you noticed by your superiors and, if you are the right person for the job, when a promotion becomes available, it will be yours.

Note those words 'if you are the right person for the job'. It is a common misconception that if you are not promoted, there is something wrong with the company. Usually the truth of the matter is that if you are not promoted, there is something wrong with you. You might not be in the wrong company. You might be the wrong person.

If you are in a company in which there is a high level of volatility and change, and if people around you are being promoted or placed in more attractive areas while you stay locked in the same position, it is time to ask yourself some serious questions. This is a time for some emotional intelligence. Remove your personal feelings from the equation and look at the situation objectively. Are the people who have been promoted better at what they do than you are in some areas? If so, what are these areas and how can the weaknesses be addressed and strengthened? Even more to the point, are you in the right line of work? Is your career path being blocked because it is a path you never should have taken in the first place?

There are many people who are brilliant at their jobs, but not necessarily suited to the next step on the ladder. They might have great work skills, but no people skills. Their talent might be more valuable to their employer as a worker bee than as a supervisor. In fact, putting them in charge of others might be counterproductive. They could be overly authoritative, they could have a manner that is a turn-off to those around them, but doesn't affect their own performance. They could be bad communicators, unable to verbalise what, as a worker, they were able to grasp and put into practice almost unconsciously. This is not unusual. It is no coincidence that the best sportspeople rarely make the best coaches. Highly successful coaches usually come from the second level of sporting endeavour, those who, while not the very best themselves, have been able to look at the best in action and break down their performance in an analytical manner. They are then able to communicate that analysis to those under their control. Ask the greatest athletes how they did what they did and invariably they won't be able to tell you. It just came naturally. Ask the best coach what it was that the best athlete in their sport did to make them the best and they will be able to tell you in point form.

If this is the case in your working life, if you are good at what you do but unsuited to telling others what they should do, it is crunch time. Are you satisfied with where you are? Will you be happy to stay there for the rest of your working life? If the answer is no, you will have to change the direction of your career. You will have to find a job in which your particular skills will be better utilised.

One of the most successful cross-overs, incredible as it might seem, is from accountancy to sales. A person might be highly numerate but unwilling to spend the rest of their working days in an office wrestling with figures. They are, to use another hack-neyed term, a people-person. They like talking to others, discussing options, giving advice – or even more importantly, listening. It is another popular misconception that the best salespeople are the best talkers. In fact, the best salespeople are the ones who ask the best questions, and then listen to the answers and act on them. Despite the apparent gulf between accountancy and sales, in fact, accountants often make brilliant salespeople. They are usually well organised and pay great attention to detail. So although the common caricature of an accountant is of a quiet mouse of a person, given something to sell, they more often than not will go about the task systematically and logically – and roar like a lion.

## ROLE MODELS AND MENTORS

We once spoke to a man who told us the first thing he did when starting a new job was 'to look around and see the person whose job I want – then go for it'. We can't recommend this sniper approach, but it is very productive to look around the work environment to find someone senior whose style and work ethic you admire, then adopt this person as a role model. There are, of course, two types of role model: internal and external. The internal role model will help you find the best way to grasp the technical aspects of your work. The external role model may be someone outside your work-life whose values you respect. The way to benefit from a role model is to ask yourself: 'What would they do in this situation?' and then follow that path. Ideally, a workplace role model will be a manager or someone who is on an upward path in the organisation. Think of them as a guide through the jungle. Follow their footsteps along the track and, all things being equal, you will avoid the quicksand and crocodiles.

The role model is different to the mentor. A mentor is more like a life coach, someone who takes you under their wing and gives advice or points you in the right direction when you ask. For this reason, the mentor will be someone you have come to know well. They will no doubt admire you just as you admire them, otherwise they would not be prepared to help you.

How to find and attract a mentor? Well, first you must identify them. They will probably be someone you are immediately attracted to. The reason being, even if you do not realise it, they are a composite of all the ambitions you have had over the years. Subconsciously you have been putting together an identikit picture of the person you hope to become. Your mentor will closely reflect that image. If the person slips easily into the role of mentor and adopts you, chances are you remind them of themselves at an earlier stage in their career. You will not be a threat to them, rather they will be happy to help you along the path and help ensure that you do not make the same mistakes they made at the same stage. How do you position yourself to be adopted by a mentor? It could be as simple as bumping into them at the water cooler and striking up a conversation. You should not be overly sycophantic or fawning. If this is to be a true mentor–protégé relationship, it will not be necessary. Chances are you will have similar aims, objectives and personality. It is just a case of allowing the relationship to evolve at its own pace. A mentor–protégé relationship usually follows this pattern: you will see someone whose style appeals to you, you will meet that person and impress them. They will ask you to fulfil a small task that you do particularly well. You will earn their respect and they will see that you are a person worth investing in.

While the mentor might be happy to unofficially appoint you as their protégé, the role model does not have to be close to you. As a matter of fact, they do not even need to know you exist. Similarly you might not even know them personally. You just have to be impressed with the way they conduct themself and do business. If they have succeeded, you can be sure that by following them, you too are likely to succeed. You should not slavishly copy them and you should not model yourself on just one person. Be selective. Choose two, three or even more role models and take from them the elements that you believe contribute to what you want to be. You might be impressed with the way one person dresses or speaks, with the way another deals with clients. You might feel one person's organisational style is ideal for your line of work. If you are a shy person who finds it hard to enter a room full of people or speak in public, watch how the most outgoing person in your organisation manages these most difficult tasks and borrow their enthusiasm and skill. Some might call it copying; in effect, it is learning from the experts around you. Imitation, after all, is the most sincere form of flattery.

## DEALING WITH CONFLICT

There is conflict in every workplace and every profession. Just as children playing in a kindergarten cannot all agree on which game to play or the way to play it, highly paid and respected workers will also disagree from time to time. Just because an employee earns a six-figure salary does not mean he or she will be able to make their way through their career without the odd tiff with their colleagues. Sometimes these will be sorted out over a cup of coffee or a drink. Sometimes they will need outside arbitration, because the fact is that conflict will never just go away. It must be faced and resolved.

The key to resolving conflict sounds simple, but is often hard. Both parties must be prepared to listen. Listen to the other point of view, assess that point of view using rational thought, then state your side of the argument clearly and succinctly. Don't jump in with what you believe to be the solution to the conflict and expect the other party to automatically accept it. The best way to get what you want is to let the other person suggest it. Easier said than done? Perhaps. Try this: put the power in the person's grasp. Say to them: 'Well, what do you think we should do to resolve this matter to everyone's satisfaction?' The key word is 'everyone's'. By giving the other party control you are in effect demanding that they compromise. The best you can hope for is to meet in the middle and by letting them lead you there, you will almost certainly achieve it.

Most conflicts come from a lack of trust, therefore when discussing a disagreement, be open, honest and frank. The other person involved might not be as open as you are, but that is not your concern. You can only be responsible for your own actions and react to the actions of others. If you become involved in a confrontation, always try to match the intensity of the other person. Be guided by their body language and tone of voice. Do not try to overpower them, just meet them. And much as it might be hard, try to understand their argument from their position, rather than your own. The ultimate aim must be to find a solution, regardless of how unrealistic, impractical or unfair you might believe the other party to be.

This is particularly true when you are clashing with a person who is in a position of authority over you. It will be hard, but you must have the internal fortitude to verbalise your feelings calmly, firmly and tactfully – even to your boss.

In the case of a peer, if you can't find a position of compromise acceptable to both sides, the matter should be referred to an arbiter – a person you both respect – who will sit in on the debate and judge the merits. This person's advice should be accepted, even if it does not totally satisfy either party. The aim is for the conflict to be resolved by a plan of action, not necessarily for there to be a winner or loser. As long as there is a resolution, rather than the dispute being left hanging, in the long run it will be a win-win situation. Doing something about the situation, regardless of how unpalatable it might seem at the time, is always going to be better than doing nothing.

## CULTURE CLASHES

There is one sure-fire way to avoid culture clashes within the work environment. If you do not fit into the culture of an organisation, do not work there. It is a matter of fact that one person will find it virtually impossible to change the culture of an organisation made up of more than five people. So, if you think the culture of a company you are considering joining does not suit you, steer clear. Choosing a place of employment is no different to any other major decision in your life, whether it be buying a new car or choosing a school for your children. If you want to spend your weekends driving off-road, you shouldn't buy a sports car and hope it will somehow develop the characteristics of a four-wheel-drive. If your child is academically inclined you would be ill-advised to enrol them in a sporting school and then expect the school to change its emphasis. It will not happen, any more than the culture of a company will change to suit one individual. Therefore, if you are looking to change your place of employment, you must be very honest with yourself on this issue. Sure, the money might be great, the perks sensational and the office could have an incredible view but . . . if the culture is not right you will never be happy, unless you are in a position to change it!

### Birds of a Feather . . .

Corporate culture is defined by the people who work there.

It is virtually impossible for one person to single-handedly change the culture of an organisation made up of more than five people.

So, where does the culture of an organisation come from? Simple: from its people. Corporate culture is defined by the people who work there. Just as birds of a feather flock together, so do similar personality types attract one another. The corporate culture is self-generating, starting at the top and working its way down through the staff. Just as, say, Microsoft and the Federal Government are totally different organisations, so too are the people who work there different. Someone who is comfortable in public service will not be comfortable in a less structured, more entrepreneurial organisation. That person will be attracted to the public service-type job and happily stay there. The entrepreneur will go to Microsoft and prosper. This is, once again, why it is so important to look at the people who interview you for a job as representative of the people you will work with if you join that organisation. It stands to reason that if the interviewers did not have something in common with others in the organisation, they would not have risen to the position they hold or even remained with the company. So, if you do not feel comfortable with the interviewers, it is a fair assumption that you will not feel comfortable with your future colleagues. This being the case, think long and hard about whether you want to take the job. After all, much as a job is just one stepping stone in a career, it is best that you stay on that stone long enough to benefit from it. And when you leave, it must be because you want to move on to the next stone, not because it was so uncomfortable you just had to jump off.

## PLAYING POLITICS

Just about every workplace is political. It might be as trivial as some people liking the food in the canteen and others wanting it changed. It could be a few workers disapproving of a supervisor's style or others not wanting to join the union. No matter how serious or seemingly petty the issue, inevitably people will take sides and much as you would like to steer clear, you will be drawn in. Even by refusing to take a particular stance, you are taking a stance. The old saying 'you either run with the hounds or the hares' is, sadly, very true. No one appreciates a fence-sitter, any more than they accept someone trivialising an issue which they hold dear. So, how do you avoid being brought down by politics? By being very, very clever.

> Staying neutral and focussing on the customer and the outputs of your job is the safest place to be within a culture that values performance.

First, take your time before aligning yourself with either side of an issue. Don't be pulled into an argument before you have had time to stand back and look at both the differing views and the people who hold them. Obviously, it is not a good move to start criticising people when you have been in a job for only a short time. You should try, without appearing to be nosey or gossipy, to learn the history of the argument. And, if you are new, be assured that any wrong moves you make will haunt you for a long time. Long-time workmates and friends will forgive each other a multitude of sins – and more often than not, when the smoke settles they will look for a scapegoat. It is often the newcomer.

So what do you do? The answer is sometimes easier said than done, but you should align yourself with the winners. Not the winners of a particular argument or intra-office intrigue, but the winners in life. If you are a positive, optimistic person, you should be close to positive and optimistic people. Look around, find the most successful, vibrant people in the organisation. That is the political party you should join.

## MEETING CHALLENGES

Some people thrive on meetings, others abhor them and simply switch off; some dominate, while others are intimidated. But no matter what you think of meetings, the simple fact of the matter is that they are a major part of business life, and they are here to stay.

So how best to shine in the meeting situation?

- First, it is a good rule not to speak unless you have something to say. Sounds simple, doesn't it? – which makes it all the more amazing that some people cannot achieve it. There are some people who simply cannot handle silence. They feel they must speak. And speaking just for the sake of speaking is where many people come undone.

- If you do have something to say, keep it brief. Hollywood movie-makers believe that the attention span of the average teenage film-goer is the length of time it takes to consume a large box of popcorn and a large drink. That's more than the attention span of a busy executive. The attention span of a participant in a meeting is closer to ten seconds – so keep it short, and keep it punchy.

- Always be on time for a meeting. There is nothing more annoying (and harmful to one's career) than arriving late for a meeting and requiring an update on what has already been discussed.

- Don't try to take over a meeting unless it is appropriate. When is it appropriate? You will have to be the judge of that, but tread warily. Taking control of a meeting is like taking control of a fully loaded semitrailer. You have to get it where you want without having an accident, stop it, and get out safely.
- Listen to what others have to say. A common trait is for people to be so keen to say something themselves that they cannot listen to what others are saying. This can be rude and worse, embarrassing, if you make a point which has already been made just as well by someone else.

## The Art of Being a Good Listener

It is said that we are born with two ears and one mouth for a reason: the ability to hear is twice as hard, and twice as important, as the ability to speak.

Why is listening so important?

Because it enables us to ask the right questions, and intelligent questions are the key to all knowledge. Ask someone the right question, and they will tell you everything you want to know.

- When you are addressing the room during a meeting, make sure you look people in the eye. If you focus on them, they will listen to what you have to say. Will they remember what you have said? That is up to you and the way you present it. Put simply, you should aim to be memorable.
- And finally, use people's first name when you address them. As Dale Carnegie, author of *How To Win Friends and Influence People*, noted: the most powerful word in the language is someone's name. Use it in conversation and they will immediately

give you their attention. Use it after not having seen them for a long time, and they will be impressed.

---

### How to Remember Someone's Name

Recalling names is an acquired skill (as much as is spelling or maths). It can be learnt with practice.

The first step towards remembering someone's name it to listen when they give it to you – not just be waiting to give them yours.

You may try to find a mnemonic to make it easier to recall that person's name. A mnemonic is a device to assist your memory. (For example, a mnemonic for William (Bill) in Accounts could go something like this Bill = Invoice = Accounts. Or Blanche is the woman wearing white = Blanche.)

If you do not trust your memory, or if the meeting is too large, spend the first few seconds drawing a diagram of the table, with names listed in seating order. It might be a trick, but it is a very valuable one.

---

## HOW TO GAIN RECOGNITION THAT YOU ARE THE BEST IN YOUR CLASS

How will you know when you are a valuable employee? When people start referring queries in your direction and pointing you out to others and saying 'I can't help you with that – but that person will know what to do.' Having a good understanding of your working environment and knowing how to get things done – even if it is not in your direct area of work – is the perfect start to gaining recognition as someone who knows their stuff. Of course making a success of your work-life is about a lot more than becoming a Mr or Ms Fixit or the unofficial Information Desk. It comes back to underselling and overachieving. You have been employed to do a certain job and if you do that job well, you will be noticed by the right people. But that in itself will not be enough to ensure that your career moves forward at the right pace. It will be the little things that set you apart. To be really successful, you will go that extra mile – but it will not be contrived or put on. You won't make a fuss or draw attention to yourself. You will find the perfect balance: neither upsetting your co-workers nor being a doormat. You will just get on with the job. As you strive to achieve your dream career, you will do the small things well, not because you think you will get something for it, but because you want to. And when that happens, you will be well on the way to making that dream a reality.

## CASE STUDY
## From Marine Biology to Advertising:
## Narelle, 42

Narelle grew up in an academic family. Her father was a university professor with degrees in three different fields. He was the dean of a college, and Narelle went through school assuming – without really focussing on the specifics of what this would entail – that she would follow in his footsteps.

> I felt very comfortable about universities. I had spent most of my life either living on campus or visiting my father when he worked there. I suppose I never really thought about it very deeply, it was just sort of understood that when I finished school I would go to further education and study something.

While the study came easily to Narelle, the 'something' that she would study did not.

My father had this philosophy, which I can see now is very old-fashioned. He used to say if you didn't have a university degree you might as well work behind a counter at Woolworths. Because of what he did and how much universities were a part of our lives, I never questioned it. The problem was I couldn't really decide what I wanted to study. Nothing jumped out at me; there was nothing I had spent all my life dreaming about doing. For two years as I tried to make up my mind what I wanted to do, I worked for the father of a friend as a receptionist and typist. Finally, I thought 'this is so boring, if I don't do something soon I'm going to go nuts'.

The only course that really interested me was science, because I thought I wanted to be a marine biologist. My father had a degree in marine biology, so it all seemed to work out well. It was only when I was midway through the course that a lecturer made me really question whether it was what I wanted to do. He said 'What are you doing this for? Unless you get top marks and are a man, you'll never get anywhere.' He made a lot of sense of course. Much of the work entails going out on fishing trawlers for weeks at a time and the people in charge just feel it is a lot simpler if everyone on the boat is male. It's a terribly sexist thing, but that's the reality of it. I realised all this, but pressed ahead, finished my course and went overseas with a friend. I thought I'd try to get a job as a marine biologist when I got back.

Looking back on it now I can see that I wasn't suited to any of the things I had gone into. My father would have liked me to be an academic, but it just wasn't for me. The same with marine biology. I suppose I was immature. For starters I had begun university two years after leaving school, so that meant I was older than everyone else in my course. I wasn't having fun because none of my friends were there with me and if I had been honest with myself I would have realised that I am a very social person. I was a lot more interested in boys and relationships and parties than thinking about a career. Being at university made it easy to avoid facing the future. I always thought I would get married and have kids, so why worry?

When she returned from her overseas travel, Narelle looked into whatever marine biology jobs were advertised, but all seemed unsuitable. She wasn't prepared to move too far away from her friends and family and the thought of leaving her boyfriend and spending weeks on a boat with a group of strangers didn't appeal.

I guess I just didn't want to do what I had trained for. I wasn't prepared to miss out on the social scene. I wanted to stay close to my friends and do all the things other twenty-four-year-old girls were doing. A friend was working in a small advertising agency and she said 'You can type and work a switchboard, can't you? We need a temporary receptionist. Come in and help us out.' It seemed like something to do while I was waiting for the right thing to come along. Pretty soon I realised it was the right thing.

Narelle started helping on reception, but within a few weeks had moved into the media area, helping plan clients' advertising schedules and booking time and space in electronic and print media.

I was a social person and by accident I had found a very social job. It was a very small agency and the people were great. We all became very close friends. There was that little bit of pressure to make the job exciting, but the main thing for me was the friendship and team spirit. The boss owned the business and the person I was working alongside was his wife. I used to get up in the morning excited about going to work. It was a lot different to how I felt about academia. Everything seemed so old and slow moving. The people I was working with were full of life. I found it very stimulating.

I know it was a million degrees from where my father was and from where he expected me to be (a million degrees from where I expected to be too), but I just seemed to fall into the type of job with the type of people that I was suited to. The funny thing is that I didn't need a university degree to do the job – especially not one in marine biology – but it probably took me getting that degree to realise what a mistake it is to go to university just for the sake of it. The best lesson I ever learnt is that the people you work with are the ones you spend most of your life with; being in the right working environment turned out to be a lot more important to me than having the right university qualifications.

# 13

# parenthood

In following the path of one's dream career, any number of obstacles and hurdles will present themselves along the way. Some you will climb, some you will go around, but few will require as many lifestyle adjustments as those brought on by parenthood – particularly, motherhood.

To work, or not to work, that is the question. In this day and age the pressures on the working mother have never been greater. With a growing awareness of the rights of the working mother and a greater appreciation of the role women play in the corporate world, companies are becoming more flexible and encouraging. But that is not to say it is easy for either the employer or the employee and, sadly, it probably never will be. The fork in the road which points to corporate success in one direction and full-time parenting in the other is, in effect, a giant question mark and no-one can tell a parent which road is the right one to take.

Only one thing is certain: it will require both employer and employee working together to ensure success. And both sides must be willing to compromise. When considering a change in one's career path, the issue of maternity or paternity leave can be a major concern.

## PARENTAL-LEAVE POLICIES HERE AND ABROAD

Individual companies have different policies, as do different countries. More than 120 countries around the world provide paid maternity leave and health benefits by law. These include the majority of industrialised countries, with the notable exceptions of Australia and the USA.

The baseline legal position in Australia is for employers to provide fifty-two weeks unpaid maternity leave with a guarantee of employment on return. Alternatively, this can be split into twenty-six weeks leave taken by the mother and twenty-six weeks taken by the father, if he can certify that he is the primary carer.

As recently as mid 2001, one Australian institution made a decision that was seen as a breakthrough in the area of maternity leave. The Australian Catholic University made headlines when it was revealed that its female non-academic staff were to receive the most generous maternity leave entitlements ever seen in Australia. Staff who had been with the university for at least two years could take twelve weeks leave on full pay and forty weeks on 60 per cent of pay. In addition male staff could take three weeks parental leave on full pay and the university said it would introduce the same entitlements for its academic staff down the track. The decision was celebrated by the Australian Council of Trade Unions, which described it as a 'move into the 21st century'.

Until this breakthrough, the benchmark had been twelve weeks paid maternity leave for the Australian public service (including those at Government-funded universities). Although this paid leave enjoyed by Australian public-service staff had been viewed as generous, in Europe such payments by private companies have been commonplace since after World War II. Private-sector companies did not resist introducing paid leave in Europe at that time because most people worked for the government and they had to compete for talent. In Australia, private companies use paid leave entitlements as a way of attracting quality staff and retaining them.

While large companies in Australia can afford to pay such entitlements, smaller companies reject moves for compulsory paid maternity leave because they say they cannot afford to pay two salaries: that of the mother-to-be who is off work and the temporary employee who replaces her.

## Maternity Leave Entitlements Overseas

When considering working overseas, it is always wise to check local law and eligibility for ex-pats. For instance, in a country such as Austria, sixteen weeks of maternity leave on full pay is provided by law, with payment through social security. Whereas in Switzerland the period provided by law is eight weeks, paid by the employer.

Countries providing the most paid maternity leave include:

- Czech Republic (twenty-eight weeks)
- Hungary (twenty-four weeks)
- Italy (five months)
- Canada (seventeen weeks)
- Spain and Romania (sixteen weeks).

Denmark, Norway and Sweden all provide extensive paid leave that can be taken by either parent, with a portion reserved for the mother.

With the role of mother as income provider on the increase it is easy to see why these countries place such importance on helping working women through their pregnancies and encouraging them to return to work.

Statistics published by the United Nations International Labor Organization show that:

- in 30% of all households worldwide women provide the main source of income
- in Europe 59% of working women provide half or more of their family's income
- in the USA 55% of working women provide half or more of their family's income
- in India an estimated 60 million people live in households maintained solely by women
- by 2010, it is estimated that about 80% of women in industrialised countries and 70% of women globally will be working outside the home throughout their childbearing years.

For overseas regulations on maternity leave check these web sites:
- USA: www.dol.gov (Family and Medical Leave Act)
- UK: www.tiger.gov.uk
- International: www.us.ilo.org

## Flexible working arrangements

In the USA, the acceptance of the Flexible Working Arrangement (FWA) is widespread. The FWA includes such measures as tele-commuting via modem, job sharing in which two or more people share the same job, and flexible working hours. A survey in 1995 found that of the 1050 major US employers, 67% offered FWAs. This was up from 54% in 1990 and no doubt has grown accordingly in the years since.

In another survey, 92 major employers reported reduced staff turnover in the three years since they had implemented FWAs. They also reported an increase in job satisfaction, morale and loyalty.

While the introduction of flexible working conditions in Australia has grown markedly in recent years, so too has paid maternity leave. The Australian Workplace Industrial Relations Survey in 1995 found that 34% of workplaces with twenty or more employees had paid maternity leave. An analysis of workplace agreements during 1998 and 1999 showed that paid maternity leave was provided for in 10% of agreements, up from 7% in 1997.

Private-sector agreements provide varying periods of paid maternity leave, generally from six to twelve weeks. Some agreements require twelve months service before maternity leave is paid, and some require the woman to return to work before some or all of the leave is paid.

So, make sure you know your legal entitlements. If, as in some cases in Australia and the USA, they are open to negotiation, try to strike a deal before you commence your employment. But much as you might be able to do this to your satisfaction, be warned: negotiating your maternity leave is just the first step. Putting it into practice is just as important.

## WHEN TO MAKE THE ANNOUNCEMENT

Another complicating issue when considering parenting and career change in Australia is the fact that women are not legally bound to reveal the fact they are pregnant at interview. Nor can an employer ask if they intend to start a family in the future.

The issue of when (or if) to reveal to prospective employers that you are pregnant is a dilemma, particularly when applying for a senior position or a middle-ranking position that you hope will lead to bigger things. Job seekers have told us of their concerns that they could be labelled as 'dishonest' by an employer if they remained silent during a job interview and then revealed their pregnancy after landing the job. At the same time, they know their chances of being successful in an interview situation will be severely handicapped if they tell a potential employer they are pregnant.

For this reason, there are those who believe that the best time to tell a potential employer you are pregnant is after the second interview when you have been offered the job. A job seeker is in the most powerful position to negotiate at the point where they have been offered the job, but have not yet accepted it.

If it is important for you to find out a company's attitude to maternity leave, then you should slip the question in during your first interview amongst a range of others relating to general company cultural issues. These could include the company's attitude to study leave, their performance review system, any career development programs and so on.

## JUGGLING PARENTHOOD AND A PROFESSION

Maternity-leave expert Michele Marriman advises that the key to a successful balance of maternity leave and work commitments is meticulous planning. Here is her advice drawn from Monster.com:

How do you balance your changing body, your changing hormones and your career? Start by planning your maternity leave early in your pregnancy. Here's how:

- *Break the news.*
  Depending on your relationship with your boss, this may be the easiest – or toughest – part of the process. Be sure to give your boss some idea of your plans and assure him or her that you'll make the transition as smooth as possible. Your message needs to be, 'I care about this job and I'm going to do everything I can to make sure things run smoothly while I'm not here.'
- *Nail down the policy.*
  In a perfect world, you'd get information on your company's leave policy before breaking the news to your boss,

but you'll probably have to talk to someone in Human Resources for specifics. Knowing how fast news travels in a company, you should talk to your boss first. Don't do it over the telephone, make an appointment with HR, so you'll have the person's full attention, and be sure to get everything in writing.

- *Consider your options.*
  As you're deciding how much time to take (or even whether or not to return at all) take your time. And remember that you may feel differently once the baby is born.

- *Write a 'how-to' program for your fill-in.*
  Put together a written job description, including a calendar with daily, weekly or monthly duties. Attach a step-by-step set of instructions, a list of helpful hints, client information and contact information. Some people put together a notebook that says 'when this happens, do this'. This is the kind of thing that should go directly to the boss. Leave things in the kind of shape where somebody else can step in and do the job while you're away. You should also do some hands-on training with the person covering for you.

- *Expect change.*
  Nothing stays the same, especially in business. When you return from maternity leave, don't expect everything to be exactly the same as it was when you left. There may be internal changes at your company or market forces may have changed the way business is conducted. Or worse – the person who covered for you has really impressed. Expect the unexpected, but remember that you have a track record. You are in a strong position because your employers know you. You are a known

quantity, so they'd rather have you than someone else.
- *The best thing is to communicate your needs and plans clearly.*
And don't forget to thank everyone who helps you along
the way.

Despite how you might feel before the birth, not every woman
wants to rush back to work after maternity leave. A recent Australian study shows that while 87% of mothers want to return to
work at some stage, 74% would prefer to work part-time – and
many will defer that decision till their children reach school age.

What does that mean for your career in an age when information technology is constantly changing the world of work? Sydney
journalist Deborah Tarrant predicts that even job designations
may have altered in your absence. Some might not even exist any
more. As she says on Monster.com:

Instead of human resources, you may be interviewed by
a manager from the human capital division. The working
environment looks different due to hot-desking, virtual
offices, videoconferencing.

Just the thought of going back to work at first can
undermine your self-esteem. If you've been moving in
a world of restricted adult access (at home with the
kids) this is understandable, but not incurable.

If you are thinking you'll never be able to keep pace
and operate quickly to perform at a professional level
in a busy office, think again. Childraising comes with
deadlines and stresses. Claudia Keech, managing director of the newly launched organisation motherInc., insists
that functioning successfully in the workplace is like
learning to ride a bicycle. Once you know how to do it,
you really don't forget.

This may be the opportunity to find a fresh direction. Do you want to go back to the sector or type of role you held previously? Your level of enthusiasm is a good indicator here. If you were fulfilled by your career, then you will be keen to resume. For many women this point in their lives is pivotal, perhaps prompting a move into a field where they can build on former experience or find more flexible work.

Know-how is the solution to lacking confidence. If your computer skills need updating, then take a course. Many colleges now offer courses specifically for women returning to the work force. Have no time, and can't easily escape the kids? Then look at the possibilities for online learning.

You might not be returning to a previous position. In fact, you could be trying to enter a whole new industry. If this is the case, make sure you research the industry you're hoping to join. Identify the key players, which employers offer the best terms and conditions (on-site childcare, flexibility, parental leave, perks). It will be helpful to know the rates of pay before you go for an interview.

If there seems to be a gaping hole in your career between the last job and the next, Claudia Keech recommends filling the space by listing the skills you have honed as a parent: expertise in multi-tasking, time and people management, for instance.

Better still, gain on-the-job exposure by asking someone you know to give you (unpaid) work experience which can be listed on your resumé.

Make contingency plans. Consider in advance what will happen if one of your children is sick; what if you need to work back or travel for business? Develop

a network with other parents, or find reliable carers
you trust.

It is important that you are happy with the care
provided for your children while you work.

Remember your job is not just something you do
to keep the refrigerator stocked and your kids in gym
shoes. It is an expression of you, so once you land
a role, try to build in some time to be part of the team.
If there are office social events, join in when possible.

Be sure your colleagues and managers understand
your circumstances – but you shouldn't need to keep
reminding them. Don't complain; it is your choice to
have children.

If you are working part-time or from home, make
sure you are included in regular performance reviews
that may, in time, lead to promotion.

Our company does not have a set-in-stone policy on maternity
leave and working mothers. We treat each case as it comes and,
happily, that has proved to be a successful way to go. In fact, the
CEO of our company provides the perfect case study of a mother
juggling the demands of a successful professional life and parenthood. Anne Hatton, who has two children, aged six months and
two-and-a-half years, says there is no one-size-fits-all answer to the
professional dilemma parenthood can pose.

Everyone is in a unique situation. Which is the main
reason both sides must be flexible. I came back to work
three and a half months after the birth of my first child,
and two months after my second, so in effect it was like
I had been away on holidays. Not much had changed at
work, but a lot had changed at home. After my first

child, I worked three days a week at the office and two days, connected to the office, at home. Between the two children I was promoted and after the second child I got back to work sooner and worked four days a week in the office.

As Anne says, all cases are unique and she and her husband have decided to do a straight role swap. The family lives a few hours from the city and Anne will stay in town, while her husband stays at home with the children. One week in three, the family will join her in the city.

My husband has a very positive view of what women do and what we can do. We sat down, gave it a great deal of discussion and made a decision to do things this way. The bottom line was that he was not enjoying his previous job and I was certainly enjoying mine. I had greater potential to achieve my professional goals, so in that way it seemed the obvious choice. I approached my employers and they agreed. I think probably the only group that has found the arrangement hard to fathom is my husband's male friends. They just can't get their heads around it. They keep asking him what he does all day.

What he is doing are all the things parents everywhere are doing, while Anne is doing everything her employers expect of her.

I think if you have certain performance goals that have to be reached and you continue to reach them, there should be no questions. At the same time, the employer must be realistic. Things aren't exactly how they were before. Whether you are pregnant or a new mother, you are a different person to who you were. It is all very well for an employer to expect an employee to achieve X, Y and Z, but that might not be possible any more. At the same time, even high achievers have to accept that they can't always do everything they used to do or at the same pace. The company should help the mother manage her own expectations. That word 'flexibility' keeps coming up, but it really is so important. You have to become more focussed and more realistic. I find I now unconsciously delegate jobs into what can be done in a certain time, and those that have to be done in a certain time. The truth is, you can't be all things to all people and there are only so many hours in the day. I am in the office at 7.15 a.m. and leave at 6.15 p.m. four days a week. I will delegate some jobs so that I can do them outside those hours. For instance, I won't go through my e-mails during my days at the office, I'll do that at home.

With Anne working from home on Fridays her home, in effect, has become an extension of the office and in the days of e-mail, Internet and mobile phone, clients are often unaware she is operating outside the CBD.

Sometimes they might hear a noise in the background and ask where I am. Other times I will be talking to someone and mention I am working from home and they will say 'Really? So am I.' I am amazed at how many women work from home. The technology makes it so much easier, but that doesn't mean it is an ideal situation. If the children are asleep, it is fine, but you cannot work with children crying or running around at your feet. That is why it would be very hard to work from home in certain situations, say a sales role. Hours have to be job-specific. If you can rearrange your hours to suit the job and your responsibilities, well and good, but it isn't always possible. And, of course, the more children you have, the harder it is.

Some people find it possible, others do not, but if the hours can be worked around the job, and vice versa, it is always worth considering. We have a working mother here who starts work at 7 a.m. Her husband has his own business, so he starts at 10 a.m. after dropping the children at school. She picks them up. In effect he does the morning shift, she does the afternoon shift and it works for them.

On the other hand, we had a single mother who was working four days a week. Without the support of a partner, she found she simply couldn't do her job or raise the children as she would like. She would always come into the office after 9 a.m. and have to be out by 3.45 p.m., but that didn't give her the time needed to fulfil her obligations at work. The result was she was always stressed, trying to catch up and one step behind where she wanted to be. In the end she had to leave. It was a no-win situation.

While that is one example of a case that did not work out, there are many that do, with parents finding a balance between the responsibilities at home and work. Anne believes there are a number of guidelines that should be followed if the equation is to end in a plus for both parties.

But even if you follow Anne's Golden Rules (over the page), she concedes that parenthood and a career are not always an easy mix.

## Anne's Golden Rules for Working Mothers

- *When considering joining a new organisation, look very carefully before making the move. Different organisations have different views of maternity leave and working mothers. Loyalty plays a big part in determining how understanding an employer will be.*

  'I had been with my company for several years and reached a certain level before I became pregnant,' Anne said. 'The company knew me and knew what I was capable of and we were able to reach a middle ground. Sometimes I think employees can expect too much. If you have been with a company only a short time and not built up the loyalty factor, it may not be fair to expect too much from the employer.'

- *Try to see things from the employer's perspective.*

  'Some people seem to think only of what the organisation owes them, rather that trying to find a way to make the situation work,' she said. 'This isn't a small thing. Your whole life changes when you start a family. In terms of a career it is important to take a long-term view, not just try to maximise your entitlements. If you want to make something work, you must make it work for the employer as well.'

- *Be considerate.*

  'I was still seeing clients when I was eight months pregnant. I would make sure I was wearing a nice outfit and that my behaviour was always appropriate. I don't think it is fair to be in an important meeting with clients and have to go outside to the bathroom every few minutes. When the pregnancy interferes with performance, it is time to take leave or start working from home. Even when working outside the office one must be considerate. When I am working at home I will not make a call if the children are making noise in the room. The client deserves your full attention, as do your children.'

I know that some working mothers are still being
harassed and victimised. They might come back from
maternity leave and find that their job has been taken
or they could be overlooked for promotion because
their employers feel 'Why bother? She's only going to
go and have more kids.' I hear examples from job
seekers who are looking to move into a friendlier area.
Again, this is why you must be very careful about looking before you leap into a new position.

If the new role involves job sharing, it is important to learn everything you can about the job, and the person you will be sharing it
with. It is unfortunate, but true, that working parents often have to
work harder than their colleagues to prove that parenting isn't
affecting their performance. They might even have to work longer
hours or take on harder assignments in order to build up 'bonus
points' for the inevitable occasions when the system will break
down and they will need to take time to fix it. With children, be
assured, it will happen, sooner or later.

And then, of course, there is the battle the working parent
wages within their own conscience. Am I doing the right thing?
Will my child suffer in the long term?

Even with a system that is obviously working and with a rewarding career path stretching ahead of her, Anne Hatton admits it is
a battle she fights regularly.

It plays on my mind every day that I don't see my children. It is one of the biggest challenges. I suppose I want
to have my cake and eat it too. I love my family and
want to be with them, but then I have to bring myself
back to reality. This is the role I am playing. I made
a decision and I have to be strong and be happy with it.

215

You have to come to an agreement with yourself – and see it through.

When she was at school, Laurel admired the creative students – the ones who could draw and design. She never dreamed she would be one of them.

'I was an academic,' she said. 'I never realised that inside this smart kid who was good with numbers and learning things was a creative type waiting to get out.'

Leaving school with excellent pass marks, Laurel enrolled in a commerce degree at university thinking it would be a good basis for going into business for herself.

'I didn't know what business I wanted to start, I just felt that would be a good thing to do. To be perfectly honest I didn't really have much idea of what I wanted to do, just that I wanted to try something.'

As she completed her course, Laurel obtained some part-time work in an accountancy firm.

I started off thinking 'This is so boring, I won't be able to stand doing this too long. As soon as something comes up, I'm out of here.' I was still there ten years later. I suppose I got into a rut. I was married by that stage and had two young children. The job just became part of my life. I couldn't get out because I could never find the time to even think about what I would do next.

Finally the decision was taken out of Laurel's hands. Her husband was transferred interstate and the family moved south.

'That was all I needed,' Laurel said. 'If I hadn't been forced to leave it would have taken me a lot longer. I still had that ambition to run my own business, but I had never been in a position to do anything about it. Now I was.'

With her husband starting his new job immediately, Laurel was left at home with the children in an unfamiliar city and circumstances.

It was the first time I hadn't had a job in my adult life. I had time on my hands, so I decided to make myself something to wear. I'd never tried anything like that before in my life. I had no background in it at all, no formal training, but I just designed an outfit and made it. Because I had always been considered an academic, I didn't think I had any artistic flair, but as I was designing this outfit it just seemed to flow naturally. It was the time when hand-painted clothes were just starting to take off and what I designed was fairly striking. It was hand-embellished and beaded in vibrant colours. Most of the people walking around town seemed to be wearing black, so I suppose I was pretty eye-catching wearing this thing and pushing a pram with two babies in it.

When Laurel wore the outfit into a clothing shop the proprietor admired it and asked where she had bought it. Laurel told her proudly that she had designed and made it herself.

She asked me if I could supply her shop with more. I said, 'Oh sure, how many do you need?' I took the order, walked outside and freaked. I had only been in town for a month, I had no contacts and no idea of where to get help. Some-how I filled the order and started supplying that shop regularly, then another and a couple more. Finally, I decided I would start selling the clothes directly from home rather than wholesaling.

With her accounting and commerce background coupled with her newfound creative talents, Laurel was able to build a flourishing business, just as she had always dreamed of. When Laurel, her husband and family moved back to their home State after a few years, she opened a shop to showcase her fashion label, which has proved even more successful than selling from home. With Laurel designing four ranges comprising forty to fifty styles each year for the past five years, it is a huge workload which sometimes has her wondering how long her creative juices will keep flowing.

I must admit a few months before each range is due I ask myself 'What will happen if I run out of ideas?' But thankfully that hasn't happened. The whole thing is amazing. I guess I was always a creative person, but because my priority was studying or passing exams and then working in a fairly dry environment I never let that side of me come to the surface. It wasn't a conscious decision, I didn't get up one morning and think 'I'm going to change today.' It was just a process of change brought on by circumstance.

And now that Laurel has unleashed the creative side of her personality, her eye for business is looking for new opportunities.

The shop has been hugely successful, but I have seen the fashion industry change a lot over the past few years. I want to remain in business for myself, but I think a few years down the track it will be in another creative area, perhaps in interior design. The beauty of finding that I had these creative skills relatively late meant that I was able to get a solid business grounding as well. I'm not sure where the two sides of my personality are going to take me next, but I am certainly looking forward to finding out.

# 14

# a moveable feast

A career is a passport to the world. In fact, a good career can take you around the world just as easily and with a lot more trimmings than any airline. Whether it is a hairdresser taking her scissors and cutting sunbathers' hair on a Greek island or a high-powered investment banker looking down on Hong Kong harbour from his luxury apartment on The Peak, the motto 'Have Job, Will Travel' can take you wherever you want to go.

Of course, when you get there, things won't always be exactly as you imagined. You will have to be at all times properly prepared and educated. You will have to fit in with different cultures, languages and local customs.

What is the best way to learn how to do business in foreign countries? One of our top staff, speaking from experience, believes you can learn just about everything there is to know by sitting in the lobby of the best hotel in town for a few hours. As he says, all the business customs will be on show. All you have to do is look and learn. How should you greet a business acquaintance? Do you shake hands or bow? What is the etiquette for presenting business cards, and what is seen as acceptable dress? How far away do you stand when greeting a business contact and how effusive or deferential should you be? It's all there in the lobby, he says. Certainly that is one way of doing a crash-course on your new place of business.

To ensure you get a job overseas and then have a smooth landing professionally once your feet are on the ground in the new place, you must offer specific expertise that an employer wants and that also surpasses local knowledge.

Consultant Allan Hoffman offers these five tips for finding work overseas through Monster.com:

1.  *Prepare a strategy.*

    You've decided you want to look for a job abroad, but what sort of job? And where? Are you prepared to live – and work – in a country with a culture and language that is different from your own? As a first step in looking for a job abroad, you should develop a strategy for your search.

    Try to get a sense of your marketability with Monster.com's 'Testing Your Overseas Job Marketability' quiz. You'll garner tips to help you market yourself for jobs abroad. Finally, be sure to read 'Five Strategies for Finding Work Abroad'.

2.  *Learn how others have made it abroad.*

    Finding a job in another country can seem like an overwhelming task.

    Are you up for it? Find encouragement from others who've done it. We've talked to lots of them, seeking their tips and advice on finding jobs abroad. You can talk to friends (or friends of friends) who have worked abroad, but we've made it easier by gathering lots of Q&A interviews with people who have worked everywhere from Costa Rica to Qatar. Look at these, not just for the personal stories, but also for tips about finding jobs overseas.

3. *Get ready for an international interview.*

   Don't expect a company to fly you to Japan or Saudi Arabia for an interview first off. Interviewing for an international job can be a vastly different experience to interviewing for work in the USA or Australia. If you're used to face-to-face contact, you may be surprised: your interview might be conducted entirely through e-mail, videoconferencing or any of the other high-tech techniques discussed earlier in this book.

4. *Enter the Global Gateway.*

   If you are truly prepared to start your job search (i.e. when you know what sort of job you want and where), visit the Global Gateway. This is the quickest route to finding international positions. Simply choose the country or region where you would like to work, click on the 'Submit' button, and you'll have a selection of jobs awaiting your perusal. Depending on the location, you may also find other resources, such as visa information and employer profiles.

5. *Ask questions.*

   Still looking? Stuck in your search? Think about visiting the 'International Jobs' message board, where you can ask our experts questions about the international job market. We also suggest www.expatforum.com as a good source of information and an opportunity to chat online with expats. Whether you want to check that your professional qualifications are recognised overseas, or how to start looking for internships abroad, you'll find an answer here.

As Allan says, and as anyone who has surfed through the web will attest, it is all there. But all-encompassing as the web is, there is still that invaluable ingredient: local knowledge.

We asked some of our staff working in centres around the world to forward information that they feel could be important to people planning a relocation. Some of the following facts and tips are available on other web sites. Most though were gathered the hard way: through trial and error, watching and listening – in and out of hotel lobbies. What follows is not a totally comprehensive guide (for more details visit Monster.com) but it does provide some priceless hints on making it overseas.

## USA

The USA is a country of contrasts, both geographical and social and this is reflected when applying for a job with a US corporation. Americans are up-front people who set great store on the spoken word. They will expect you to be the same way. To win the job you must be assertive and a self-promoter, however if you appear too aggressive or self-congratulatory you will go to the bottom of the list – such is the delicate balance of the US employer–employee relationship.

### Job applications and the interview

US employers will expect you to provide either a letter of application or a resumé. The letter of application is a one-page, error-free, concise and attractive outline of relevant job experiences, skills, accomplishments, and academic credentials. The resumé is a detailed chronology of academic and formal work experiences. If you are sending these documents via mail or e-mail prior to your interview, they should be accompanied by a cover letter. Demonstrate your knowledge of the company in this letter.

Tell your interviewers why they should hire you. Always be positive about your past experiences, supervisors, and co-workers, but at the same time be careful not to overstep the mark. Unless presented as what was part of a group project, citing past accomplishments and skills can be viewed as boastful, self-serving, or too individualistic.

You should follow-up with employers after the interview; telephone inquiries about the status of your application and thank-you letters are acceptable practice.

As far as self-disclosure is concerned, American interviewers will be particularly probing, so be prepared to outline your experiences, hobbies, strengths and weaknesses and to answer questions related to personality, such as leadership style and problem-solving abilities. And, of course, be prepared to answer questions related to your immigration status.

American interviewers will expect you to show a strong measure of career self-awareness. You will need to demonstrate knowledge of self, career goals, and how they relate to the job. You will also be expected to know about the organisation that is interviewing you. Some US firms like to use the job-interview process as a form of market research into the organisation and how it is seen in the community. Do your research and give thoughtful answers. If there is something about the company or its products that you do not like, touch on it, but also give suggestions about how these weaknesses might be fixed. If there is something about the company and its products that you particularly like, make sure you mention it.

Give a firm handshake when introduced to people and greet them by name – Americans are very big on the use of first names, as anyone who has ever tried to deal with a large US public utility will know. So, it is imperative that you remember the names of the people in the room and use them whenever you address them.

You should arrive anywhere from five to fifteen minutes before your appointment and call if you need to reschedule or will be late.

## US dress codes
Where American companies were once the home of what was known as the 'button down' look, with dark suits, white shirts and mirror-shined shoes being a veritable uniform, the accepted look

is now what is called 'business casual'.

In recent months, firms such as Morgan Stanley Dean Witter, J.P. Morgan, Goldman Sachs and Credit Suisse First Boston have instituted full-time casual dress policies, joining companies such as Coca-Cola, Ford, General Motors, Andersen Consulting and Sears, where casual dress in some cases has been the norm for years. One workplace that is still holding out is the Federal Government. Representatives at the White House and the FBI indicate that 'business professional' is still the policy.

'Business casual' means different things in different companies, so it is wise to contact the Human Resources department at specific firms to learn about their dress guidelines. Ask yourself 'What is the office culture?' 'What's my role in it?'. Once you start the job you could also look at a supervisor whose style you admire for guidance.

Here are some general rules for women. Wear one smart item (blazer, wool skirt) with one of your basic wardrobe items (trousers, sweater). Stick to solid colours and clean, simple shapes. Add interest with accessories, like a scarf. Acceptable shoes include loafers, low pumps and low sling-backs. Complete your outfit with a roomy, practical, up-to-date handbag.

For men, business casual generally means khaki slacks, polo shirts, slip-ons (or 'dockers') and a sports jacket.

The next level up is termed 'business appropriate' (meaning the clothes should fit the particular occasion) and 'business ready' (meaning a traditional suit is sitting in the wardrobe ready to be worn when needed).

At least on the East Coast, guidelines call for clothes to be 'in good taste'. This means no denim, spandex, jeans, moccasins, sandals, team logo shirts, shorts, halter tops, tank tops, leggings, sweat suits or tracksuits and no provocative or revealing clothing of any kind. In general, T-shirts are not recommended, though a recent newspaper article reported on their newfound versatility, at least among Manhattan shoppers. For women, T-shirts are trendy, yet inexpensive, and the more up-scale versions are showing up in offices.

## HONG KONG

Hong Kong is an upbeat and vibrant city where businesspeople work hard and smart, take chances and enjoy every minute of it. New arrivals are quickly infected with its exciting spirit.

The metropolis works extremely well. The public transportation system is among the best and the crime rate is among the lowest of any of the world's major cities. Medical care is excellent. Modern supermarkets and purveyors of fine food and wine sell delicacies that may be ordered online. In all categories the shopping is excellent. The expatriate lifestyle is cosmopolitan, to say the least.

Hong Kong has a subtropical climate. Temperatures rarely dip below 10 degrees Celsius (50 degrees Fahrenheit) and the annual mean temperature is 23 degrees Celsius (73 degrees Fahrenheit).

### Domestic help

Parents arriving in Hong Kong with children of pre-school age will find it quite straightforward to set them up with live-in caregivers or at a pre-school or play group. The executive lifestyle in Hong Kong includes affordable, live-in domestic help. Specialist recruitment agencies can source domestic helpers with particular strengths to suit individual needs, including professionally trained child-carers, nurses or cooks. Most executive-style flats and houses include domestic-helper quarters.

Helpers work six days per week, with official holidays off, at a minimum wage equivalent to $942 per month, under a standard two-year contract. Expatriate employers who are very satisfied with the quality of their helper's work often will pay more. Hiring a domestic helper usually takes from six to twelve weeks and requires completion of visa paperwork with the Immigration Department, so it is advisable to start immediately upon arrival in Hong Kong.

## Accommodation

Hong Kong offers a wide variety of housing options and residential lifestyles within reasonable commuting time to the main office districts. Couples and singles often settle near Central District to be within walking distance of work and restaurants, clubs and nightlife. Beachfront communities that are within an easy commute of Central District are favoured by families with small children. Many high-rise complexes offer resort-like facilities and self-contained residents' clubs that include swimming pools and gymnasiums.

Each of the leading residential neighbourhoods favoured by corporate executives has their own distinctive appeal:

- Victoria Peak (known as 'The Peak') offers a cool, quiet parkland environment and easy access to jogging trails and picnic spots, as well as some of Hong Kong's leading international schools, a leading private hospital and up-scale dining and recreation at The Peak Galleria complex.
- Mid-Levels is a high-rise residential area with immediate access to the offices of Central District, dining out, nightlife, shopping and schools, as well as some breathtaking views of Victoria Harbour. Many commuters take a ride to work each morning on the unique 800-metre outdoor escalator that connects Mid-Levels to Central District.
- On the south side of Hong Kong Island, Repulse Bay offers both high-rise and low-rise blocks, good shopping, the Hong Kong International Junior School and the longest sandy beach on the Island. Other south-side neighbourhoods offer individual houses with gardens, low-rises and proximity to some of Hong Kong's exclusive private clubs.

- Discovery Bay, on Lantau Island, has a fine sandy beach with a golf club, residents' club and easy access to trails through Lantau's country parks. A short high-speed ferry ride from Central District, Discovery Bay is also only twenty-five minutes by tunnel and road to Hong Kong's international airport.

Families arriving in Hong Kong have a variety of temporary housing options. Many hotels offer long-term accommodation in the form of larger rooms or suites with self-catering facilities. Serviced apartments are becoming increasingly popular. These are regular apartments that are maintained by the building's staff and are leased on a month-to-month basis. Amenities to look for in serviced apartments include clubhouse facilities, indoor and outdoor swimming pools, on-site supermarkets, shuttle bus service and optional maid services.

The world's leading international property consultants and corporate relocation specialists have offices in Hong Kong. Services include comprehensive property searches, lease renewals, rent negotiations, valuations and full orientation packages. These services can greatly facilitate the search for short-term and long-term residential quarters. Leading property and relocation consultants have web sites with information specific to their Hong Kong activities. A comprehensive source of information is the Hong Kong web site www.firstchoicehongkong.gov.hk.

## Interviews

The dress code for men attending interviews is a smart business suit. For women, the rules are less stringent and conservative than in other major Asian centres (for example, wearing open-toe shoes is acceptable).

When handing out your business card, use both hands and bow very slightly from the neck.

In Hong Kong, as in the rest of Asia, you have to be sensitive about a person's age and position, especially if they come from a more traditional background and from a more traditional industry, such as the banking sector. Thus you would need to address Alan Chan, as 'Mr Chan', as opposed to 'Alan'.

Punctuality is not as important as in some centres. It is not unknown for people to be late or to be kept waiting for a meeting. This is acceptable up to a reasonable amount of time.

## Resumés

The prospective employer will want to know what value you will be adding to the organisation. You should display a certain level of cultural sensitivity in your resumé and show your adaptability to the local market. It is of major importance that you highlight any Asian language skills and if you have had any experience working with cross-cultural groups.

## Meeting culture

When the person you are meeting enters the room, you should stand up, offer a firm handshake and then exchange cards, which should be printed in English on one side and Chinese on the other. While passing the card to more traditional clients, you hand it to them with the Chinese side up; for the less traditional clients, the English side up is fine.

A handy piece of advice is to respect your intuitions. In a market as complex as Hong Kong, there are few hard and fast rules and a lot of grey areas. The Chinese can be an enigmatic race, but are very tolerant of, and willing to adapt to, newcomers. Words such as '*gweilo*' meaning 'white ghost' in Cantonese are not meant to be derogatory, they are merely used to differentiate between local and overseas people.

## Eating culture

Eating is a ritual in Hong Kong as in most parts of Asia. Many business deals are conducted over lunch. In a traditional Chinese meal, when pouring tea, it is polite to pour the tea for the other people on your table first and yourself last. Do not be surprised if the older generation tap the table twice while you pour tea – it is their way of saying thank you. Do not be embarrassed if the locals laugh at your ability to eat with chopsticks – they do not mean to be rude. Most locals are very adaptable to Western habits, so don't be shy to ask for a fork. Do not mind if people talk with their mouths full – it is very common in Hong Kong.

If you are served the fish head or tail, feel honoured. It signifies a good start and good end to your relationship. If you do not wish to eat it, refuse diplomatically.

Lunches are much longer affairs than in Western culture and they are used to cement relationships. People generally do not skip lunch, as this is the time they catch up with their colleagues and exchange information. Most entertaining is done at an outside venue rather than in the home since most people live in small flats. Usually the husband and wife both work so it is more convenient and time-saving to dine outside.

Tea drinking is more a part of the local culture than is alcohol.

And a word of warning: what Westerners might view as rude behaviour is, in some cases, common practice in Hong Kong. Burping before, during and after meals is normal and spitting is not unusual.

## Doing business with overseas clients

A difference between East and West is that more business is conducted over lunch. More people work overtime, since the pace of business is fast and, while it is common in the Western world, Asian businessmen do not entertain at night with their partners.

## Pros of Relocating to Hong Kong

- A tax rate of 15%
- Affordable domestic help
- Good food
- Close to South-East Asia, offering opportunities to travel
- Cultural vitality
- Good climate in winter.

## Cons of Relocating to Hong Kong

- Small apartments
- Language difficulties
- High pollution levels
- Not enough open space
- High cost of living
- Less outdoor activity
- High humidity.

If invited out at night by your Asian colleague or host, don't assume that your spouse or partner is included in the invitation.

### Dressing for success

Hong Kong is a very brand-conscious market. The underlying motto is: if you've got it, flaunt it. And don't think that the label or brand-name of the clothing you are wearing is not noticed by your Asian counterpart. It is, and is stored away. Note that the wrist-watch is a status symbol. Hong Kong businesspeople will automatically notice the type of watch worn by the person they are doing business with and often will comment if they are impressed.

At work businesspeople should appear neat and tidy. Shiny suits, unironed shirts and a messy appearance are definite no-noes.

Women should not wear as much make-up as they do in Western countries – beware of the humidity.

## JAPAN
### Resumés

Japanese resumés are still handwritten on a standardised form. However, for non-Japanese people, a typed Western-style resumé is acceptable. Make sure you attach a passport-style photo.

The actual content of the resumé is almost the same as in the West: your name, address, telephone number, job history, professional qualifications, language and other skills. However, there are a few points that differ. Asking for your age in Japan is not illegal and indeed you are expected to give your date of birth on the resumé as a key piece of personal information. Some more traditional companies may even require brief details of family members (their names, ages, occupations). The reason for this is to avoid hiring anyone with unseemly connections to things such as criminal elements or anything that would hurt the company's reputation.

There is also a section in the resumé where you can write about how excited you are about the service and products the prospective company provides. Of course, do not forget to tell them how wonderful and professional you are. A hard copy mailed to the company is still much preferred over e-mail.

### The interview

In Japan an interview starts long before you ever sit face to face with the interviewer. The interviewee is expected to arrive at least ten minutes before the set time. On arrival, there is usually a receptionist who is the first hurdle to overcome – give a nice bow (at an exact 45-degree angle), a greeting and introduce yourself, explaining who you are to see. Remember to smile nicely, as the receptionist may well be screening you too. You will then be shown to the interview room.

The room usually has a table with chairs all around, from which you can take your pick. The correct place is to sit facing the door so that you face the interviewer as they come into the room. Once you have been told to make yourself at home, take a seat but never make yourself look at home despite insistence that you do so. Take the most appropriate seat and keep a good posture with back straight. Never use the chair's armrest and try not to make use of the chair's comfort.

The receptionist will still be tending to you and will bring you a drink whilst you are waiting for the interviewer. At this point, despite your nervous thirst, it is important not to touch the drink. Say thank you, but do not drink until the interviewer has come in and prompts you to do so.

When the interviewer enters, stand up and have your business card at the ready. The correct procedure is as follows: first give a bow at a 45-degree angle and then, maintaining eye contact, say 'My name is X, thank you very much for your time. It is my great pleasure to meet you.' You then offer your business card with both hands, and bow again.

The interviewer will reciprocate and try to give you their business card. Do not take their card until yours has been taken first – this is an important rule to show respect. To receive the card both hands should also be used, all the while of course, maintaining your 45-degree angle. You may then sit down, placing the interviewer's business card on your business card holder on the table in front of you.

At the end of the interview, you bow again and thank the interviewer for their time. The interviewer usually accompanies you to the entrance to see you out, where you bow and give your thanks once again. If the departure point is the elevator, bow to the interviewer until the elevator doors are closed.

And remember that this entire procedure is just as important as the content of the interview itself.

## Meeting culture

It is often necessary to approach a Japanese company with an introduction, as they are reluctant to respond to cold calls or unsolicited letters. This is usually done with the help of a third-party intermediary, who is somebody known and trusted by the target company.

Preferably, send a team rather than just a sole representative to meetings in Japan. The team members should have a range of rank and responsibility. Try to keep the same team members from meeting to meeting – this will help to establish long-term relationships.

Business cards are essential in Japan; bring a large supply of good quality cards, preferably with a Japanese translation on the reverse side. Giving gifts is also very important in Japan – it shows respect and helps to build good relationships. Bringing things such as local souvenirs or items with the company logo shows an appreciation of this tradition. The guests traditionally present their hosts with gifts towards the end of the first visit.

Having your own interpreter ensures no bias and also helps with meeting preparations.

Meetings are where the Japanese corporate culture can be best observed. Everyone is expected to be on time at internal company meetings no matter how crazily busy they are. Once again, seating positions are critical: juniors are near the door, seniors further away. This becomes very important the higher the meeting level. Communication is never as direct as in the West, with an emphasis on using formal Japanese and an obvious show of respect for seniors. In addition, there is a traditional tendency to use fewer words than we do in the West, which often makes meetings rather unclear and difficult to understand. Traditionally, the ideal worker is one who does a perfect job with little to say, which may seem paradoxical when the very point of a business meeting is the exchange of information to produce new ideas and strategies.

In Japan you need to be able to read between the lines to understand what people really mean. Differences in communication style are often the source of business failings. The Japanese are indirect and humble, using polite, non-confrontational forms of expression. Try to adopt a more indirect, courteous, non-aggressive style. Recently, however, there have been tremendous changes towards more direct, meaningful meetings.

Allow enough time for meetings – Japanese managers often take much longer with the meeting process than would be the case in the West. It is important not to rush things and it is probably counterproductive in the long run to do so. Do not try to hurry the getting-acquainted phase by moving too quickly into a business discussion. The first meeting is more about building a relationship than selling a product or service. Much more time than in the West may be given to small talk before moving on to business matters.

Give and receive business cards with both hands; and treat any that are handed to you with great respect. Seating is never random in Japan, either in business or social situations. Allow your 'opposite number' to direct you to your place. Learn the opposition team hierarchy and also ensure they understand the ranking of everyone on your team. Since there are relatively few female managers in corporate Japan, a Western businesswoman must make her title and authority clear to the Japanese team at an early stage and underscore it throughout the meetings.

A lot of the meeting time may be devoted to the exchange of information. The Japanese are extremely thorough and will want presentations supported with solid facts.

During negotiation and agreement phases of meetings ensure that the entire team is united behind any proposals or concessions that you make. Also give the Japanese side time to reach an agreement amongst themselves and bear in mind that this process cannot be rushed.

Avoid the impulse to break the periods of silence that often occur during meetings in Japan. Though they might seem uncomfortably long by Western standards, they are a normal part of Japanese non-verbal communications.

## Eating culture

Eating culture, especially at business occasions is of great importance. It is advantageous to take part in any after-hours socialising – informal gatherings are an important part of business life in Japan. These will help strengthen relationships and also may give you off-the-record inside information, such as how the meetings are going and warnings of any potential trouble areas. If you are invited to dinner, you as a client should order the best, expensive dishes – never order the cheap dishes or courses. This would be considered rude as it implies your host is not making enough money.

Once the meal commences, never touch anything until invited to start. Of course, there will be beer and sake as well. The etiquette with drinks is for you to always pour and top up your hosts' glasses. He or she will then fill your glass. Always pay attention to the state of the glasses, and never allow your host to fill their own.

Mastering chopsticks is a bonus and will become a topic of conversation no matter what your level of skill is. The major no-noes are to stick chopsticks upright into the rice (this is done when presenting offerings to the deceased) and also to pass food from your chopsticks to another's (a ritual associated with funerals – involving the passing of cremated bones).

The main idea of eating together is to get to know each other and build a closer relationship. Enjoy yourself, but never forget it is a business occasion. The Japanese may drink a great deal, but they still remain aware of the underlying business purpose.

### Honne, tatemae and giri

'*Honne*' is a person's true feelings and '*tatemae*' is what the individual or group presents to the outside world (the public stance). This can explain why the Japanese sometimes appear to have contradictory viewpoints. An understanding of these concepts will help you to reach positive outcomes.

'*Giri*' (mutual obligation) is a bond in business and personal relationships. If you have received a favour from someone, you are expected to reciprocate in the future. *Giri* is often expressed through the giving of gifts that will strengthen the relationship and increase mutual respect.

### How to Succeed in Japan

- Proceed slowly.
- Focus on long-term business relations.
- Preserve a congenial atmosphere.
- Be less verbose, and use silences and pauses.
- Observe good communications skills, such as monitoring feedback, active listening, and decoding body language.
- Allow the Japanese to save face.
- Accept Japanese ambiguity and delays.
- Utilise non-business social settings.

**Holidays and travel times**

Avoid making business trips during major holiday periods. These include New Year's celebrations (first week in January), Golden Week (a series of various public holidays held between 29 April and 5 May), and the Obon Festival (this Buddhist religious festival is when many Japanese return to their hometowns to visit ancestral graves; depending on the region it occurs between 13 July and 15 July or 13 August and 15 August). Also be aware that the Japanese fiscal year ends on 31 March, and that as the end of the fiscal year approaches no long-term projects are started.

The large cities of Japan, such as Tokyo and Osaka, at first sight appear to be teeming concrete jungles and will seem quite daunting. Despite the apparent sprawl, it is a surprisingly ordered chaos. The public transport system is world-renowned for its efficiency and with some study is relatively easy to use to move around (particularly in central Tokyo). Trains and buses, the latter a little trickier to use, are cheap and plentiful. Taxis however are expensive and given the complexities of the address

### Managing Time Zones

| | |
|---|---|
| –07:00 | Los Angeles |
| –04:00 | New York |
| +08:00 | Hong Kong |
| +08:00 | Singapore |
| +09:00 | Tokyo |
| +10:00 | Sydney |
| +00:00 | GMT |

*Note:* There is no daylight savings time in Japan.

system and street layout are often difficult to use. Despite being very clean and operated by polite drivers, they can be quite a challenge for non-Japanese, especially with destinations off the beaten track. Consequently, be sure to leave plenty of time for travel to and from meetings.

## Dressing for success

Men should go by the general rule that one wears a suit no matter how hot and humid the weather. The only variable is colour, with light-coloured suits being acceptable in July and August.

As far as women are concerned, many wear some form of uniform. This does not necessarily mean they work for a department store since a lot of women (often called OL or 'Office Ladies') are to be found working in administration roles in traditional Japanese companies and banks.

In general, for women, the dress code for success does not differ that greatly from big cities worldwide. However, stockings are still regarded as an important part of the total outfit and most Japanese companies expect their female employees to wear them every day, regardless of the weather. Make-up, like stockings, is an essential part of the dress code. It is considered impolite if a woman does not put on make-up when meeting a client or indeed for day-to-day office duties.

## Relocation

When visualising apartment living in Japan, think small – very small. That way you won't be too shocked when you submit yourself to the rounds of the *Fugosanya* – (apartment rental shops) and finally squeeze into your new home away from home.

Though the floor space is meagre, unfortunately the financial outlay is not. To take possession of an apartment you will need to hand over two months' rent as deposit, another two months' (non-returnable at the end of the lease) as key money and up to another two months' for the contract. On top of that, there is a management fee charged at the discretion of the agent. For example, if the rent is 150 000 yen a month (around $3000) your initial payment will be approximately 900 000 yen ($18 000). To enter into an accommodation contract requires you to have a Japanese guarantor who will be held liable for any damage or unpaid rental fees.

The cost of living in Japan is high by Australian standards. A quick trip to the corner market will cost around $80 for one medium-sized bag of daily provisions. There are a number of small markets catering to foreigners (such as National Azabu, Kinokuniya, Meidiya and Peacock).

## CHINA

For so long the 'closed shop' of Asian commerce, China is now opening its borders to international trade. But this does not make it another Hong Kong or Singapore. It is still a matter of steady as she goes, so international businesspeople hoping to do business with, or relocate to, China must be patient and prepared to follow time-honoured practice and customs.

To prepare for an interview, go to the company's web site and study the company background first. At the interview, be sure to listen carefully. Unlike in some cultures, the interview is not a place to ask a lot of questions.

Your resumé should clearly state your skills and qualifications, experience and achievements. The employer will want to know what sort of person you are, but this will be deduced from your professional background, rather than from personal statements.

In business meetings let the most senior participant start first and guide the meeting. Shanghai business culture has a strong sense of seniority, and the more junior members of the firm would never speak over their boss or try to monopolise the conversation.

There is only one time zone in China: Beijing time.

China might have the world's largest population, but individualism is not encouraged. Therefore, dress in a professional and neat manner, but try not to wear anything that will make you stand out in the crowd. More sedate colours are the norm.

When filling a position most employers would prefer the local People's Republic of China job seeker to avoid high relocation and interviewing costs. Someone being brought to China from another country will always have unique skills or product knowledge. The Beijing Olympics in 2008 will be one way that international experts, such as consultants from the Sydney 2000 experience, will be invited to work in China.

Cost of living in China is determined by a system of 'tier cities'.

- First-tier cities (such as Beijing, Shanghai, Guangzhou and Shenzhen) are the most expensive, which is reflected in the higher salary and benefits packages offered in these areas.
- In second-tier cities (such as Tianjian, Nanjing, Hefei and Chengdu) the cost of living will be 20% to 30% less than first-tier cities. This will be reflected in the salary package.

## LATIN AMERICA

Considering the image of Latin America as an easy-going society, the business dress code is quite formal, with suits and ties for men and 'power suits' for women.

Interviews in Latin America are also more formal than in Australia or the USA, with less small talk and discussion about hobbies and outside activities unless it is related to community work and social responsibility, which is becoming more important. With no government restrictions, the interviewer may inquire about personal details that would be illegal in Australia.

Resumés will be expected, as in the USA, to give a full personal and job history as it relates to the job being offered. A handy hint is to bring plenty of business cards as they are handed out freely.

There is more physical contact between friends and associates than in European-based societies, with pats on the shoulder and hugs for good friends. One kiss on each cheek is the acceptable form for greeting a woman and a handshake and perhaps a tap on the shoulder for men. And do not be surprised to see children at social events. Latin Americans do not leave their children with babysitters, parents bring them along.

Meeting culture in Latin America is very much in contrast to the formal interview situation. Before getting down to business, there is more socialising and storytelling than in the USA, Britain or Australia. It takes more time to get into the heart of the matter.

Lunch and dinner are later and longer. Office hours are also longer. There is very little alcohol consumed with lunch.

In major cities, private international schools are available for expats, and the cost of living is cheaper in Brazil than in the USA or Europe.

Time zones in Brazil are only one or two hours ahead of New York.

## CANADA

### Resumés and interviews

Interviews will not differ much from those in the USA. At a job interview, the employer will ask questions about education, skills, and work experience. Often employers ask questions such as: Why do you want to work here? Why are you the best person for the job? Tell me about yourself.

Employers want you to explain your skills. They expect you to show interest in their business. It is a good idea to practise answering questions before the interview.

Bring a hard copy of your resumé to the interview, as well as a list of references, so that you can produce a copy of them if requested.

It is also a good idea to follow up a day or so later with a letter or email thanking the interviewer for taking the time to meet you.

Like Australia, Canada has strong legislation about what can and cannot be asked at interviews regarding such areas as ethnicity, religion and disability. For instance, a Canadian employer cannot ask directly about a prospective employee's citizenship, age or family commitments. Certain questions relating to fluency of spoken and written language can be asked if the answer is relevant to the performance of the job. Others, such as whether the job seeker would be willing to travel, relocate or work overtime, are allowed as long as they are asked of all job seekers.

The two main types of resumé used in Canada are the reverse chronological and the functional.

- *A reverse chronological resumé* is the most commonly used. This type of resumé includes your most recent work history, then goes backwards in time. Related accomplishments are provided for each job you have held.

- A strong *functional resumé* creates a profile of your experience based on skill groupings, irrespective of any particular jobs held while attaining them. A functional format works well if you can provide skills groupings and accomplishments that relate to your new career objective.

The only drawback of the functional resumé is that it is not as widely accepted as the chronological resumé. This can be overcome by creating a functional format, and then also including a listing of company names, position titles, and dates in reverse chronological order (in abbreviated form) at the end of the resumé.

Do not include information in your resumé about your date of birth, number of children, or marital status.

Generally, it is an asset to include both French and English translations on your business card. Moreover, if you plan to do business in the province of Quebec, ensure that your card is translated into French. Business cards are exchanged, although not usually during an initial greeting.

Many, though not all, credentials from other countries are acceptable in Canada. To get a job or more education, your certificates may have to be translated and evaluated. The Open Learning Agency (OLA) operates the International Credential Evaluation Service (ICES). ICES will assess foreign secondary and post-secondary certificates for employment.

To work in Canada you need a Social Insurance Number (SIN). Most immigrants apply for this number shortly after arriving in Canada.

If Canada turns out to be where your dream job is to be found, everything you could possibly want to know about relocating to Canada can be found at www.relocatecanada.com.

## Not the USA

Although they are not overtly nationalistic flag-wavers, Canadians usually hope that visitors will recognise and appreciate the many unique attributes that make their country distinct from the United States. Canada is a multicultural society and the customs of businesspeople may reflect their ethnic background.

In Canadian business culture, consciousness of rank and title is somewhat more pronounced than in the USA. In business situations, maintain good posture and an air of formality.

In most cases, meetings are essentially democratic and all participants are allowed to express their opinions. Agreement tends to be sought rather than imposed.

Negotiating styles are frequently similar to those in the USA, although the pace may be slightly slower. When doing business Canadians like to deal in fact, rather than relying on gut instinct.

Generally speaking, Canadians are polite listeners and will rarely interrupt a good speech or presentation. Moreover, many Canadians excel in courteous give and take. A good sense of humour is almost always a welcome attribute, however Canadians do not have difficulty saying no. Although decision-making can be highly individualistic, company policy must be followed at all times.

## Eating culture

Business meals are popular in Canada and in most cities there will be a variety of good restaurants from which to choose. Breakfast meetings are becoming common as well. Business lunches are usually short (an hour or so) with lighter foods and often no alcohol.

In general, it is acceptable to be fifteen minutes late for an evening social engagement. Do not, however, be late by more than thirty minutes. When invited to a dinner, the best policy is to wait for your Canadian host to bring up the subject of business.

Invitations to dine at a Canadian home are relatively infrequent and should be considered quite an honour. When you visit a home, a gift of flowers, candy, wine or liquor is usually welcome. If you are a guest in a home, wait for permission from your hosts before wandering from room to room. A few days after a dinner party, a telephone call or note thanking the host or hostess is a thoughtful and appreciated gesture.

Make a point of offering any main dishes to others before serving yourself. The fork is held in the right hand and is used for eating. The knife is used to cut or spread. To use the knife, the fork is switched to the left hand or is laid down; to continue eating, the fork is switched back to the right hand. If you prefer not to eat something, simply decline politely.

Restaurants charge a Goods and Services Tax (GST) of seven per cent. Gratuities are not included in the bill, but you will be expected to tip fifteen per cent for good service. Restaurants in Canada often have smoking and non-smoking sections. In an increasing number of Canadian communities, however, there are by-laws in effect prohibiting smoking in restaurants and bars. With the exception of the streets, you will find that smoking is restricted in most public places.

## Dress codes

Professional dress codes in Canada do not differ greatly from what is acceptable in major centres such as London, Paris, New York, Sydney or Hong Kong. Comfortable, tasteful clothing is the norm.

A conservative, well-dressed appearance is important in Canadian business culture. Your clothing does not necessarily have to be brand-new or trendy. Wearing quality clothing that is old, but presentable, can be perfectly acceptable. Some professions allow for casual dress, but it is best to err on the formal side when in doubt. Suit and tie is standard attire for men, business suits or dresses for women. Pantsuits, in classic styles, can also be acceptable. Accessorising, which adds flair to even very simple outfits, is also a common practice. In rural areas and small towns, clothing tends to be more informal and there is not so much emphasis on appearing fashionable.

Canadian winters can be cold and dressing warmly is essential. During this season ensure that you bring a coat and pair of gloves. It is also a good idea to take a pair of boots with good treads to help you walk with ease through the ice, snow and slush you are likely to encounter on the pavement. Moreover, selecting a well-insulated pair of boots can help protect your feet from the often intense cold. During their leisure time, Canadians dress casually

## Managing Time Zones

| | |
|---|---|
| −03:30 | (Newfoundland Standard Time) Newfoundland |
| −04:00 | (Atlantic Standard Time) the Maritime Provinces and Labrador |
| −05:00 | (Eastern Standard Time) Quebec and most of Ontario |
| −06:00 | (Central Standard Time) Manitoba, the northwest corner of Ontario and eastern Saskatchewan |
| −07:00 | (Mountain Standard Time) west Saskatchewan, Alberta and a slice of northeast British Columbia |
| −05:00 to −07:00 | (Eastern Standard Time to Mountain Standard Time) the Northwest Territories |
| −8:00 | (Pacific Standard Time) the Yukon and bulk of British Columbia |
| +00:00 | GMT |

*Note:* Canada has six time zones, but only 4.5 hours separate Newfoundland from British Columbia.

Daylight saving (when the clocks are put forward one hour) is in effect in all regions except Saskatchewan and northeast British Columbia from the first Sunday in April to the last Saturday in October.

and items such as jeans, T-shirts, sweatpants, shorts and running shoes are acceptable in public.

Canadians in general do not wear scent in a business setting. Perfume, aftershave, and heavily scented personal care products such as shampoo and hairspray should be avoided, or at least used sparingly. It's often believed that perfume is worn to cover up poor personal hygiene. Furthermore, the presence of scent can also be a health hazard to individuals with asthma, which is a relatively common condition in Canada. Consequently, many jurisdictions in Canada forbid the wearing of scented products in hospitals and doctors' offices.

## THE UK

European citizens may live and work in the UK free of any immigration controls. Citizens of the USA, Canada, Australia, South Africa and New Zealand are generally allowed to stay six months without a visa.

London is one of the world's great financial centres and a leader in many professions and fields of endeavour. For this reason it has always been a magnet for those people wanting to gain experience, further their careers, and live and work in an exciting city at the gateway to Europe.

Historically, Britain's major regional cities have also been recognised as world leaders in specialised industries. This is still the case and a period spent working in cities such as Manchester or Liverpool will offer professional experience available nowhere else in the world.

### Finding a job

As with all overseas career moves, there are two ways to secure a job in England: either apply for and be offered the job before leaving your country of origin, or travel to England on spec and apply for jobs once you arrive. In the first case, the best way to find, apply for, and gain a job in England is through one of the leading web-based employment services such as Monster.com. There are a large number of British firms specialising in executive relocation to the UK. These are listed on the Internet under 'Business relocation to UK'. Most offer a full service, including travel, transport of personal items, homesearch, schoolsearch and notification of change of address to banks and utilities. Several also offer multilingual services. They will identify available positions and put you in contact with a recruitment professional who will help you to apply. If you are successful and accept a position, you will expect that details such as travel arrangements, help in finding accommodation and the setting up of financial matters will be arranged for you. At the very least, all relevant information should be made available before and after you arrive in the UK.

For those who prefer to seek work once they arrive in the UK, there is full-time and casual work. The latter arrangement will allow more time for you to travel and track down your dream job. In both cases, the best option is to register with one of the many large and reputable employment specialists, such as TMP World-wide, which operates in the UK.

Looking for work in the UK is not dissimilar from seeking employment in any of the other English-speaking Western countries of the world. The format for an English resumé is straightforward and similar to that expected in the USA, Australia and Canada. Your experience, educational achievements and qualifications should always be presented in reverse chronological order. Be aware that employers in the UK do verify qualifications, so if you have started a course or professional qualification and not yet completed it make that very clear on your resumé. UK employers are accustomed to employing overseas nationals and will recognise your qualifications and educational results. It is advisable to always take a copy of certificates or degrees with you to an interview, along with a hard copy of your resumé.

Your experience, listed with last job first, should include exact dates of employment, the company name, country of location, and type and size of company. (Remember a major company in your country may not necessarily be a household name in the UK.)

Employers in the UK will want to see your job title, your core responsibilities and your achievements included on your resumé.

The easiest way to present this is in bullet-point form. If you find yourself writing long sentences – STOP! Short succinct bullet points will convey your point far more affectively than a long-winded paragraph. You will have an opportunity to expand on these points during the interview. Also a reminder that, although all of your experience is relevant, it is your most recent that you should be spending the majority of your time and space on.

The UK does not yet have age discrimination legislation laws, therefore most employers will expect to see your age given on your resumé. If you are not comfortable with supplying this detail, feel free to omit it. In line with other countries though, you are not obliged to put marital status or number of children on a resumé. You are also protected by law from being questioned about these issues at interview.

Having applied for a position be prepared to wait up to two weeks to receive notification or a response. The UK is gravitating towards a standard of two or three interviews before offer stage. This is not a rule across the board, but be prepared for the fact that you are unlikely to get an immediate answer following one interview.

## The interview

The first interview may well be with an individual from Human Resources. They will assess your resumé and conduct a reasonably informal interview. The next interview will probably be with a Line Manager, or someone who would be your senior. This will generally be a more formal interview where your skills and background will be discussed in more depth.

Be prepared for competency-type interview questions. For example, instead of being asked simply what you believe your skills to be, you may additionally be asked to talk the interviewer through at least one occasion when you have demonstrated these skills.

In other words do not claim to have a skill that you cannot back up!

The employer will usually call for references before, or just after, a verbal offer is given. Make sure that your referees know that you have named them. A speedy response from your referees can move you to a formal offer stage much more quickly.

An offer letter will cover your terms of employment and your remuneration. Benefits in the UK can include private health care, a company car and a pension. Any discussions about salary that you have will be about an annual amount before tax and national insurance. It is always worth asking what your take-home pay will be. Some companies may offer performance-related bonuses. These may be discretionary and may be paid quarterly or annually. These bonuses will also be subject to tax.

## Dress code

At interview, as with actual work, you will be expected to present yourself in business attire. Across the board this should be a suit and tie for men, and a suit for women (trouser, skirt or dress). In line with many US companies, a majority of London-based firms may well have a dress-down Friday. However, do not assume this and check before ditching your suit once a week! Also 'dress down' usually means 'smart casual', so no jeans or training shoes.

If the company you are going to differs from this dress code and has a more casual approach you will be told at interview. It is always safer to err on the side of caution, therefore a dark suit may be deemed more appropriate for job interviews. Remember, however impressive your resumé is, the interviewer will make many assumptions based upon what they see when they meet you, so make sure you are presenting your best side.

## The National Insurance number and banks

In order to work in the UK you will need to get a National Insurance number. This ensures that the correct amount of tax and National Insurance is deducted from your salary. Without a National Insurance number your salary will be deducted at the emergency rates, which are much higher than the standard rates. To get allocated a National Insurance number you must arrange a meeting at your local office. The National Insurance Hotline telephone number is 020 8258 8855.

To get paid you obviously need a bank account. Getting a bank account in the UK involves getting a written reference. If you sign up with a recruitment agency they can normally supply you with the necessary reference. Alternatively, if you are doing casual work, it is normally easy to get a bank account if your employer will write you a reference.

All international banks have branches in London, but they are not all easily accessible. It is wise to transfer funds into a local bank as soon as possible. The largest British banks and building societies include Barclays, Lloyds-TSB, National Westminster (NatWest), HSBC and Abbey National. You will need 'walking around' money before your first pay cheque. Travellers' cheques are widely accepted in English banks. Buy them in pounds sterling to avoid changing currencies twice. Change bureaus in London frequently levy outrageous commissions and fees, so make sure you establish any deductions in advance. The bureaus at the international airports are exceptions to this rule, charging less than most banks and cashing sterling travellers' cheques for free. Cashpoints (ATMs) are very common in Britain: most are linked to major credit cards as well as the Cirrus, Maestro and Plus cash networks.

### Surviving in London

England is extremely expensive and London even more so. While in London you will need to budget at least $70 a day for the barest survival until you start your job. If you stay in a hotel and eat restaurant meals you could easily spend $180 a day without being extravagant. Once you get out of the city the costs will drop.

If you eat in an English restaurant you should leave a tip of at least ten per cent unless the service was unsatisfactory. Waiters are often paid low wages on the assumption that their income will be supplemented by tips. Some restaurants include a service charge on the bill, in which case a gratuity is unnecessary.

### Transport

Britain prides itself on its public transport and information is readily available. Learning to master the system is one of the best investments you can make whilst working in England. Getting around London and other major cities is done very easily using the wide range of excellent public transport that is available. The London Underground runs from 6 a.m. to midnight every day of the year, excluding Christmas Day. Trains run frequently and are the quickest and cheapest way to travel around London.

As well as London's major Underground system, smaller specialised rail systems (such as the Thames Link servicing selected stations around London, and the Heathrow Express, which takes fifteen minutes to whisk you between Heathrow Airport and Paddington station and runs every quarter of an hour) offer reliable, economic alternatives to the often overcrowded and slow road system.

London's bus system can take a lot longer than the Underground, due to the volume of road traffic. Buses normally run every ten minutes or so. If time is not of the essence, the bus system is an efficient and economical way to see some sights and get your bearings. Buses run throughout the night and can be caught from Trafalgar Square to sites all over London.

Major British cities, such as Liverpool and Manchester, also have outstanding public transport systems.

The other way of travelling around London and major cities is the taxi. The best known of these is the traditional black London taxi that charges via the meter system – but be warned: the meter fare is not all you are expected to pay. British cabbies expect a tip of at least ten per cent and will often become angry if they do not receive one. Another form of transport is the Mini Cab. These are unmarked cars, which you pre-arrange to hire with a driver, negotiating the fee beforehand.

## KOREA

Expatriate life in Korea is interesting and rewarding. There is a lot going on, much to learn and many opportunities to make lasting friendships. In addition, the expatriate businessperson must become their company's expert on Korea. There are historical, cultural and political events constantly unfolding that must be understood in order to effectively manage the local venture. Expatriates are ambassadors for their home countries and this unique position presents opportunities to meet people and hear informed views on many interesting and worthwhile topics from a variety of perspectives.

### Pre-arrival assistance

Potential expatriate business people will find it helpful to familiarise themselves with the many worthwhile publications that exist pertaining to Korea and to Asia in general. Periodicals include the *Korea Times, Korea Herald, International Herald Tribune, Far-Eastern Economic Review, The Asian Wall Street Journal, The Korea Economic Journal, Business Korea* and *Korea Business World.*

Korea has professional relocation-assistance companies that can help find suitable accommodation and schools, can assist in the hiring of maids and drivers, can advise on cultural training and what to bring to Korea and can alert you to quarantine requirements – all prior to you actually relocating.

## Post-arrival assistance

Once you have arrived in Korea there are many sources of information to be tapped. Some of the most promising sources are:

- Chamber of Commerce
- embassy
- law firms
- accounting firms
- Foreigners' Community Service (FOCUS)
- professional relocation-assistance companies
- members of the foreign community
- members of the Korean community.

## Korean food

Korean food can be either very delicious or leave you feeling that you may not want to experience it ever again. Korean food ranges in taste from bland to extremely spicy since many dishes are seasoned with red pepper. Koreans eat *bop* (rice steamed on its own or with other grains) as a staple, but it tastes so bland that it is accompanied by *kimchi, kuk* (soup) and other *banchan* (side dishes). *Kimchi* (a fermented food) is an essential part of the Korean meal. Basically, it is made up of Chinese cabbage seasoned with red-pepper powder, salt, garlic, ginger and a few other ingredients. A very popular type of *kuk* is *taenjang kuk*. This soup is made of *taenjang* (soybean paste), tofu (bean curd), various vegetables and sometimes meat. A popular *banchan* dish is *pulgogi* – seasoned strips of roasted beef or pork. *Pulgogi* is very popular with Westerners.

## Cultural norms

Due to the extraordinary growth of the last forty years, Korea has become an important player in the international business arena. Korea is strategically located in the world's new growth area with an abundance of energetic and skilled workers. As more and more international firms are joining with Korean enterprises, and global interdependence is becoming an inevitable reality, better understanding between East and West is vital to continued mutual prosperity. Even though Korea has undergone a rapid transition from an economy based on agriculture to one with a sophisticated industrial base, it retains a traditional value system based on Confucian philosophy, which can sometimes put it at odds with international norms. Add to this the fact that Western businesses are typically unaware of how to deal properly and effectively with their Korean counterparts and sometimes the results can be disastrous. Often this could be avoided through preparation and cultural education beforehand.

Westerners working in Korea can be caught in a dilemma. First, they have to conduct business in terms familiar to them-selves, and on the other hand they must make sure their manage-ment techniques are suitable for the country they find themselves in. Adding to the complexity are the dramatic and rapid changes in Korean political and business structures since the economic crisis of 1997. The new environment offers both opportunities and pit-falls for Westerners doing business here. The former goalposts on the Korean business and political playing fields are being moved, so that, for a while at least, both Korean and foreign business-people must negotiate new territory, removing some of the home-field advantage that has been used effectively by Korean firms in the past. It is crucial that the foreign businessperson pays close attention to the sometimes daily changes in order to understand the effects they will have on business.

One of the first things that the expatriate businessperson must learn is how Koreans act and how the Government of the Republic of Korea operates, first due to the pervasive role of government in business affairs, and then because processes and practices may differ from your expectations.

A source of confusion and frustration to newcomers is that current Korean practices often differ from stated Korean policies, so the newcomer must soon learn that they cannot wholly accept the publicised objectives of the government at face value. This was always true, but since early 1998 that divergence has been exacerbated by the economic and political events associated with the Asian economic crisis of late 1997. In the turmoil that followed Korea's request for International Monetary Fund assistance, the implementation of the IMF's program and the election of the new president, a number of significant changes in policies were enacted. The number and scope of these changes have been enormous and are likely to continue for some time. A certain amount of disappointment and confusion in matters pertaining to government and business bureaucracies is to be expected. If a foreign businessperson expects to conduct business in much the same way as in the home country, there will be a rude awakening.

## A complex web of institutions

The Korean Government cannot be treated as a single organisation. This is also true of Korean ministries, agencies and business organisations. The current administration undertook to simplify the Korean bureaucracy, but the process of change often makes the organisational structures even less easy to understand, especially for a newcomer. In the end, many of the old rules will be retained, so no matter how simple a transaction might seem to be, one will find oneself dealing with many national and local agencies at several levels, in addition to various bureaucratic subdivisions.

For example, even if an agreement has been negotiated and signed with a Korean corporation, say, in the energy field, the Ministry of Commerce, Industry and Energy must first determine the merits of the project or venture. The level of profits or dividends and matters of taxation and foreign exchange bring in the Ministry of Finance and Economy. If the venture involves construction, then the Ministry of Construction and Transportation will also need to be involved. Also, very basic to all significant ventures, the Ministry of Finance and Economy must generally support whatever scheme is proposed and rule on its 'fairness'. Finally, overseeing all of these intricate dealings, the Secretariat of the Executive Mansion (the Blue House) keeps a watchful eye and can influence the progress and course of approvals. Each of these agencies has the power of veto.

Furthermore, the foreign businessperson must deal with several levels within each agency, and each level will often interpret government policies and regulations differently. These interpretations may differ from time to time, and each agency representative may try to achieve some renegotiation of portions of an already 'signed and sealed' agreement, usually to the disadvantage of the foreign company. Each level of each agency also has a measure of veto power.

Finally, when all approvals have been obtained and the venture starts operations, the foreign businessperson may discover, sooner or later, that some of the provisions of the agreement so carefully clarified and documented may suddenly be considered no longer applicable because of 'new circumstances', 'changed conditions' or 'earlier misunderstandings'. At that point, the negotiation process will start once again. In addition, the expatriate will find that new rules and regulations are promulgated frequently, and that interpretation of both new and old rules and regulations will often vary. Again, this process may be accentuated by the economic restructuring under way since early 1998. It is advisable, therefore, for expatriates to build a certain degree of flexibility into their contract negotiations to account for possible restructuring down the line.

Remembering that the sense of the deal is more important than the letter of the contract will help to prevent frustrations. One way of doing this is to minimise concessions during the initial round of negotiations to ensure that there is still scope for agreement later. Nevertheless, the situation is that the foreign businessperson in Korea is in the position of trying to build a solid business structure on a loose foundation of as yet unconsolidated interpretations by shifting personalities! Many foreign businesses have proceeded despite these uncertainties and many have had satisfactory results, whereas inevitably others have been disappointed. It is important for every businessperson to try to understand the structure and functions of the elements of the Korean Government and to try to fathom the cultural differences that motivate incomprehensible policy.

Not only is it particularly important for each foreign businessperson to know their Korean partner and be known by him (and it usually will be a 'he' rather than a 'she'), but both partners must also know and be known in the halls of Korean Government. In this regard, the Westerner should carefully observe the interpersonal relationships at work and at social gatherings. Where the majority of Western business executives fail is in preparing to equip themselves with an awareness of basic rules that govern business conduct in the East.

For example, when Americans face contract violation few seem to realise that bringing the Korean partner (or client) to a court of law is, at best, extremely unpleasant and usually ineffective. Resorting to litigation – or even threatening to do so – is viewed in Korea as something that educated people refrain from doing.

It is a last measure to be taken only when all else fails. In Korea, resorting to the law is an indirect admission that the parties lack the personal ability to solve problems themselves. It also signals the end of a relationship.

Korean business culture is based on the Confucian ideals of moderation and harmony in interpersonal relationships. The influence of Confucianism means the adoption of a personal value system that associates the impersonal law courts and other institutional dispute-settlement techniques that are common in the West with a corresponding estrangement between people and the disintegration of essential relationships.

## Relationships in Korea

All business and social dealings are structured on a very personal basis. The relationships between the parties can be even more important than the substance of a contract. Many large dealings in the Korean business world are transacted on a handshake and no more. Honour is very important.

Westerners tend, however, to have lawyers write contracts covering every possible contingency and expect these documents to be enforceable for their full stated term. This is fine if the relationship between foreign and local partners is well established such that each feels comfortable with the other and with the deal. If one has not spent the time and effort to establish that relationship, and if it is not maintained, one may find that contracts are disregarded in certain vital aspects or that protracted negotiations on certain points ensue, causing inevitable frustration. It is thus essential that the potential investor allows his front-line manager (expatriate or local) the opportunity to establish these relationships before and during the launch of the venture in Korea. The manager should also be involved closely in the government approval process. To have the paperwork completed by lawyers remote from

259

Korea gives little opportunity for the manager to establish the relationships that will make his or her role much more effective.

While it may be in conflict with the policies of the company and/or with the personal wishes of the manager, a two-year stay in Korea is often not long enough to build up the key relationships and take advantage of the benefits they bring. Often a manager will just get into their stride with their associates after two years, only to be moved and replaced at the time of greatest potential productivity. While Korean managers, for cultural reasons, are well equipped to establish relationships in Korea, expatriates must learn to adapt to the system. First, they must appreciate that it is a vital part of their role. Secondly, they must rely on someone to advise them of their obligations and responsibilities. They must be prepared to spend time, for the faster they try to proceed, the greater will be their frustration. A direct line of communication is required with the potential partner, and this should be used to its fullest if managers are to be successful in implanting ideas and requirements in the mind of the local investor.

An added tool in breaking the cultural barrier is the knowledge of some basics of the language and culture. Although most expatriates have found it impossible in their spare time to acquire enough Korean to conduct a substantial business discussion, a few polite phrases can go a long way towards establishing a good relationship with your Korean counterpart.

## Business partners

Notwithstanding the fact that the local partner has successfully courted the overseas investor and genuinely seeks a connection, his intention will most likely be that the business should be run as his own personal company. The joint venture becomes an extension of his own operation – part of his family.

It is difficult for the foreign investor, even if they have majority shareholding, to become a fully accepted member of that family. It will pay, therefore, to establish written policies and procedures very early on in the partnership, especially if non-Korean practices are to be employed. Particularly for a minority shareholding position – where a form of the Korean approval process is going to be used requiring sign-off at every level – it will help immensely if the overseas manager is formally included in the approval chain, so that all important decisions will require their personal signature.

## Head office

Relationships with the overseas head office may be strained at times when unpopular decisions must be made against the local partner's wishes. Decisions that may be reached in a matter of minutes or hours in other places can take days or weeks here. Everything is negotiable, even items that were previously discussed at length, agreed, and recorded. It is imperative that the expatriate manager considers the people at head office. Those people influential to the operation must make every effort to learn about the Korean way of life and conducting business. Be aware however that limited contact (say, an annual visit of two or three days' length) can be misleading, particularly as Koreans are extremely gracious hosts. The expatriate manager who is left to deal with the daily realities after the VIPs have departed must accept the challenge of educating the overseas head office – and if they do so the rewards are significant. It is very easy for the director or head office vice-president dropping in for a short visit to get the impression that life in Korea for the expatriate revolves around the bars and restaurants of first-class hotels.

## Staff

Relationships within the company are also critical. When hiring staff, considerations of age, educational background and

birthplace are as important as the level of education and technical ability. To employ the person with the right technical credentials but the wrong background could prove to be disastrous for
internal office harmony. A Korean's first action when employed
is to seek their level within the office or factory environment. To
establish who are their seniors (those to whom deference and
respect must be shown) and to seek out those who will defer
to them is very important, whether these people be in the
employee's own department or not. The employee cannot feel
comfortable until this task has been accomplished. Once this has
been done and the employee has become a member of the team,
then that team's harmony must be of constant concern. The
expatriate can only learn of the importance of this through experience. In the meantime, the overseas employee must rely on a
trusted member of staff to direct and advise them.

A very important category of relationship is that between the
joint-venture company and government. These relationships, like
those in the private sector, are based on personal relationships
between the key individuals in the various ministries and agencies
and those in the company's staff. Thus, the Korean partner's decision as to which individuals will be assigned to staff positions in
the joint-venture company and who will have responsibility for
government relations will be crucial in establishing relationships
with government. The seniority and background of those individuals will be an extremely accurate indicator of the level of priority
given by the Korean partner to the joint venture as a whole. If the
Korean partner is in a minority position, however, or the venture
is small in relation to the overall scale of the partner's affiliated
operations, this priority may be too low for the necessary government relationships to be effectively established. Thus, the foreign
partner may be forced to take the initiative in building government relationships in certain cases, although the Korean partner

is always more effective in this regard if they are willing to invest the necessary time and effort.

> ## CASE STUDY
> ## From Lawyer to Entrepreneurial Business Owner: Gary, 44

It was in a police station at midnight that Gary realised he did not have the necessary experience to practise criminal law. A lawyer in a general practice, who had two years experience in a wide range of areas, he decided it was time to specialise.

> I had done most things: property, conveyancing, some business sales transactions, commercial law, litigation and some criminal law. It was the criminal law that interested me most and I thought I would like to specialise in that area.
>
> Then one night I got a phone call at about 11 p.m. A client was at the police station and needed help. I went down there and he had been accused of rape. There I was, 22 years old, trying to make decisions about a man's life. I thought to myself 'What do I know?' I could give him advice – I had the legal qualifications – but I didn't have the experience. I could tell just from that small exposure to police and the system that things didn't go according to the textbook. If I was to be a successful criminal lawyer I would have to get a lot more experience. Obviously when people's lives were at stake it was important I knew what I was doing. I suppose I wasn't prepared to spend the time acquiring that knowledge, so I started looking in other directions.

The side of the business that Gary had enjoyed almost as much as criminal law was corporate law and so he began to explore his options.

He saw a press advertisement for the position of company secretary for a major financial organisation, applied and was offered the job. The position involved being chief in-house legal officer, secretary to the board, executive assistant to the CEO and liaising with external legal advisors.

It was primarily a legal role and I found it pretty dry. Essentially, with the co-operation of the CEO, I engineered myself into the position of running the branch network. I was out of law and into sales and management. I was responsible for all retail operations of the branches.

With that move, Gary had gone from practising law, to advising on law, to no law at all, but he says the grounding he had in legal practice has helped him in every other move he has made.

The legal training gave me a sense of order, of how things work. But it was the four years I had at the financial organisation that was really the most valuable experience I could have. I was managing an operation with a $30 million to $40 million budget, dealing with 500 employees – mainly women – with various levels of commitment; dealing with all kinds of eventualities, such as the trauma of robberies, all in a fairly political environment. The board were largely political appointees and dealing with that and the workings of a large and competitive retail operation was a good testing ground. It helped me find out what I was capable of doing and what I wanted to do.

Where I am now is a geometric leap from where I started, but I see it as a linear progression. I now know I needed every bit of experience I had along the way to enable me to deal with what I am doing.

Following four years with the financial organisation Gary spent seven years in corporate management roles. The last was as CEO of a company that ran a number of medical centres. The company had been started by an entrepreneurial doctor who didn't have the necessary management skills to run such a fast-growing operation, but still had a strong sense of ownership. While Gary soon found such a situation invariably leads to a clash between CEO and owner, it also provided invaluable insights, as he is now in a similar position: owner of a flourishing company who has appointed a CEO to handle the day-to-day operations. His time at the medical centre company also opened his eyes to something else: the business opportunity that he has since capitalised upon.

As part of my job I spent a lot of time travelling, seeing how similar operations were run overseas. One thing I noticed was how many Australian physiotherapists were working overseas, particularly in the USA. I investigated and found out that Australian physios are particularly well trained and proficient in comparison to their US counterparts. They are highly sought after there and particularly well paid by Australian standards. The reimbursement for physios under the US health insurance system is many times what it is in Australia under Medicare.

Gary did his sums, realised there was a demand in the USA for Australian-trained physiotherapists and decided to service the market.

I went into it with a degree of optimism. I have a friend who is married to a physiotherapist and they had set up their own practice in the USA. I decided to go into it on a larger scale. I felt if I could set up centres over there that showcased the skills of Australian physios it would generate business.

It has done that and more. He started in a Southern State with a population of five million, but which can be crossed by car in one day.

Even if the reimbursement was the same in Australia, the tyranny of distance would make it impossible to offer a similar service to such a large population. In the States we can cater for so many more people in a much smaller area. Pretty soon we had carved a niche market. We met a need and found there was a huge demand.

In a very short space of time, that one centre had grown to ten. There are plans for six more on the drawing board and expansion into two more States. And while the original plan was to import Australian talent, the company has now begun training locals, bringing them up to Australian standards.

With such a rapid expansion, Gary's gamble has obviously paid off financially, but he says money wasn't the motivation.

Money wasn't an issue at all. Initially it was the interest and excitement. It gave us the opportunity to live in another country and to test my skills without the patronage of anyone else. For the first time in my career I was the master of my own destiny. It had got to the stage where I hated working for large corporations, where I was often hamstrung from doing what I wanted to do. I know that is the way big organisations are, but when you are involved in a board meeting and a good opportunity gets shelved for political reasons it can be very frustrating. For the first time I had control over my future and the chance to select what I wanted to be involved in.

Money is a consequence of success, but it is not everything. There is only so much you can spend. Some of the corporate jobs I had in the past paid very well, but that didn't mean I felt fulfilled doing them. I look back on them now and you could pay me $1 million a year—more even – there is no amount of money you could pay me to do that sort of work again.

# 15
## Q & A

Questions, questions, questions. The life-altering decision of whether or not to make a major career move is all about questions: asking the right ones and getting the right answers. As we have said throughout this book, there will always be employment professionals, friends, family and acquaintances willing to offer advice. Take it all on board. Weigh up all the information objectively, do not take one person's viewpoint as law – ask for a second opinion. And do not make any giant leaps until you are entirely comfortable about doing so.

To help you take the first steps in your journey, here are some of the most often asked questions about career change.

*Am I better off following a career path with my current employer or looking for opportunities elsewhere?*

The fact that you have to ask this question suggests that there is something or someone blocking the way at your current job. A career is a succession of jobs, whether it is with one employer or a number of different employers. Therefore, to have a successful career the path you follow must be free and clear of impediments.

Look at your current situation. Is the next step obvious? Can you see where you want to go, and is anything stopping you from getting there? Is there a person occupying the seat you would like to be in, and if so, how long will they be there? Are there impediments, issues, or people that make your current position unsuitable? Is there a realistic chance any problems will be solved in an acceptable time?

Let the answer to these questions be your guide. If you are happy where you are and believe your career path will take you where you want to go, then by all means stay. If not, start looking around. There is an old saying: there are two ways to get to the top of a tree; one is to climb it, the other is to sit on an acorn. It is particularly true in relation to a career. You may know what you want in terms of position, title and conditions and, if you wait long enough, you might achieve them all. You might also be offered a new job and be able to negotiate those terms and conditions at the outset. This could cut years off the waiting process.

### How long should I stay in a job before I can move on?

Ideally, stay for a minimum of two years. With people now having, on average, eight different jobs in a lifetime, the stigma attached to change has all but disappeared. Of course, this does not mean that a prospective employee will be impressed with a job seeker whose resumé indicates they are a serial job hopper. As we have said, employers are looking to employ people whose job skills are suited to their company. They will want to know you have been able to acquire those skills along the way. They will not be impressed if it appears that you have not stayed in your jobs long enough to learn your supervisor's name, let alone any specific skills. There is also the consideration that filling a position and training a new employee is a time-consuming, expensive exercise. Employers will not want to go through this process too often and would invariably prefer to hire someone with a proven track record for staying put. Therefore, if possible, stay for a 'respectable' time.

If this is not possible, when applying for your next position you might want to list two previous jobs together on your resumé, for example: *June 1999–August 2000: Sales representative ABC Industries and XYZ Incorporated. Achievements during this period included* . . . In some cases it is best to use a functional resumé, which lists your skills and the highlights of previous positions, rather than giving a job-by-job chronological history. While at some stage you may still have to fill in an employment history, your first objective is to be granted an interview. When you are face to face with your prospective employer, emphasise your interest in a long-term position. Always accentuate the positives.

### Should I find a new job before I leave my old one?

Ideally, yes. While this is not always possible, it is always better to be looking for a new job from a 'position of strength'. Prospective employers will look favourably, even if subconsciously, at someone they are 'winning' from a competitor. There is always a feeling that 'if XYZ wants this person, they must be good'. From your own point of view the security of an existing job will make it easier to make the right decision. Taking a new job becomes a matter of choice, rather than urgency or even necessity. You are better placed to weigh up all the pros and cons without financial or social pressures.

Of course, this isn't always possible. You may be forced to leave your current position before you can find somewhere to go. If this happens, look at the positives. You will be free from the unsatisfactory elements that have prompted a move. You will be able to devote yourself entirely to looking for the right position, instead of fitting it into your busy work schedule. You will be able to take a short break in order to clear your mind, and you will not have to hide your job-search from those around you. This in itself can be empowering. Whatever the situation, make it work for you.

### Should I take calls from headhunters in office hours?

Yes, you should—but what you do about those calls is entirely up to you. In a recent survey taken by TMP Worldwide we found that over 63% of Australian male workers and 37.7% of females would take a call from a headhunter during work hours. Only 1.5% of males and 5.5% of females would refuse the call altogether. Once you have taken the call, it is a case of determining your next step. You can ask the recruiter to call you at home, you can call them back at a time that is more convenient (e.g. during a lunch break, after hours or on the weekend). Whatever you decide, the important factor is to make contact. You may have no intention of making a career move, but it doesn't hurt to know what is available, and how you are valued on the open market. You might be the most loyal employee in the firm, but you cannot predict the future. There are takeovers, mergers, downsizing, so remember the old Scout motto: Be prepared.

### When is the best time to make a career change?

The best time for change is when you feel ready for it. As we said earlier, you should give yourself an assessment every two years or so. Ask yourself whether you are getting from your job everything you want and need. If the answer is no, it is time to start setting new goals and looking for ways to achieve them. As far as age and personal circumstances are concerned, this is a very difficult question to answer. There is no perfect age at which to change; age is just part of an overall picture. You may be young enough to have the energy, drive and independence to make a move, but do you have the experience and maturity needed to make it a success? You may have the experience, but your family and financial commitments might make the risk too great. When the time is right, you will know.

### I know where I want to go, but how can I get there without experience?

The fact that you know what you want means you are a lot further along the path than you realise. Some people go a lifetime without ever defining a goal. What you have to do is convince an employer that your

passion and hunger is worth rewarding. Again, it gets back to
emphasising the positives, rather than dwelling on the negatives.
A functional or skills-based resumé would allow you to highlight that
you are, for example, 'hardworking' and 'able to learn new things quickly'.
You should also consider expressing a willingness to accept difficult or
less desirable conditions as one way to break into a field and gain
experience. For example, 'willing to work weekends and evenings' or
'able to travel or relocate' may open up some possibilities that might
appeal to an employer. Make sure to let the prospective employee know
of anything you have done that could provide the skills necessary for the
kind of work in which you are interested. You might not have had paid
employment, but it is surprising how many adaptable skills are learnt in
life through such activities as volunteer work, school and community
activities, sport, family responsibilities, education, Scouts or Guides or
school military cadets. No matter how long the process might take, try
not to get downhearted. Remember, the best skills you have to offer
an employer are your enthusiasm and willingness to work.

### I have been out of the work force for years. How do I get back in?

This is not unusual. What you have to do is to show a prospective
employer that just because you dropped out of the work force doesn't
mean you have dropped out of life. If you are returning to the industry
in which you used to work, demonstrate that you have kept up-to-date
with changes. This doesn't mean you have to monitor the industry on
a long-term basis. A brief refresher course will be sufficient to bring your
previous skills up to par. Attend trade conferences, take an online course
and use modern terminology in your resumé.

If it is not a case of returning to your previous industry, but trying to
enter a new one, the same applies. Do your research. Find out what the
job entails and be prepared to demonstrate that your skills are suitable
to that industry. You don't have to be in paid employment to improve
your skills. The skills you acquire as a full-time parent or overseas traveller

can be just as marketable as those picked up over years in the same job. If you have been out of work because you raised a family, continued your education, cared for a sick family member or recovered from an injury, be sure your tone is not apologetic. There's nothing wrong with being out of work for whatever reason, and a negative attitude might affect your chances of gaining employment.

### How do I decide what direction to head in?

It all gets back to self-analysis. Work out what you want in a job and find one that satisfies those requirements. Sit down and write a list of ideal job conditions:

- In your ideal job, do you want to spend a lot of time with people, with data, with words, with things?
- Would you like to work at home, in a fancy office, outdoors, at a university or somewhere else?
- Do you like to spend time with arty types, computer nerds, sports jocks, business people, hands-on types or social animals?
- Can you stand the prospect of night work or long periods of travel away from home?

This information will help paint your job profile. If the right job doesn't jump out immediately, there are books and employment specialists to help you to join up the dots. Being honest with yourself in assessing your career targets is the first step towards achieving your dream career.

### I want to make a career change that might be seen as a downward step by some people. How do I stop my qualifications being a disadvantage?

This form of inverted snobbery is not as uncommon as you might think. Sometimes people have followed a certain path just because it is expected of them, not because they are truly suited to it. Eventually this will become obvious and they will make a major change in direction.

This may require them to go backwards before they can go forward. If you are willing to accept jobs where you may be deemed overly qualified, consider not including some of your educational or work-related credentials on your resumé. And be prepared to explain, in the interview, why you do want this particular job and how your wealth of experience is a positive and not a negative.

### When is it too late to make a change?

In theory, it is never too late. That old adage 'you are only as old as you feel' applies to careers as well as to other parts of life. Without changing your perception of what you are capable of, you'll never make a success-ful career change. It may require some retraining, it will definitely take some willpower, but changing careers late in life is definitely possible.

Ideally, the experience and knowledge you have gained over many years will mean you do not have to start from square one. One of the reasons older people resist change is because they are intimidated by it. They see the way that the work environment has changed and watch young people mastering technology they have not dreamt of and think they are locked out. This does not have to be the case. Youth is not a prerequisite for learning new skills. Of course, there will be a learning curve to any new career you try, but this is the same whether you are 25 or 55. You should accept that getting proficient in new skills may be frustrating and difficult, but this doesn't make it impossible. In some cases, older people make better students. They are less easily distracted, more able to focus on a goal rather than fitting it into a number of conflicting issues like an active social life or relationship problems. The mere fact that an older person takes on a new career is proof that they are serious about what they are doing.

### I am certain that I want to make a career change and know the direction I want to take. When should I act?

Now.

# 16
# it's never too late

The path to a dream career can lead in any direction. The first step can be taken at any time. There is no limit to where a career can take you just as there is no age assigned to when you must take that first or last step.

One of the things we have learned in the years we have been helping people achieve their dream career is that a true dream never dies. As we said in the first pages of this book, the dream that leads to your perfect career can start in childhood. It can be the result of an interest that began before you can even remember. It may have started in the school playground, been suggested by a book or television documentary that worked its way into your subconscious. Where it came from and when is not important. When you decide to follow that dream is not the most vital issue either. Some people are able to turn their dreams into reality easily and quickly. They take the first steps along the path before they have even realised it. A hobby or an interest turns into a bit of pocket money, then an income and, almost inexorably, a livelihood and finally a career. For others it is not so easy. Life gets in the way. You can find yourself taking a job to earn a bit of money or to see where it leads or until something better comes along. Before you know it, the years have passed and the things that have come along include a few children and a big mortgage.

Our advice? Don't despair. Sure, work for that pay cheque, pay those bills, but never close yourself off to the opportunities that can, and will, present themselves. Don't give up on your dreams and they will never give up on you.

One of the most satisfying parts of being in the business we are in is to help people reacquaint themselves with those dreams. Sometimes they might feel they are a long way from achieving them. They might feel they have been separated from their dream by the years or have grown so far apart from them that they will never meet again. Not so. If your dream – and your resolve – is strong enough, if you are prepared to take those first steps along the path, then no matter how old you are or how far you have travelled in another direction, there will be a way.

Remember: it's never too late.

## CASE STUDY
### From Stenographer to Teacher:
### Win Walker, 80

At 80 years young, Win is living proof that the door to a dream career doesn't necessarily swing open on day one. And neither is it ever slammed shut. Sometimes it just takes a while to walk through.

It was during the Great Depression that Win was forced to leave school two years before she was due to sit her Leaving Certificate. Her family needed her to start earning a living and her dreams of teaching music, therefore, had to be set aside. To many people this would have been seen as an opportunity lost. To Win it was just a dream put on hold.

I wasn't allowed to stay for Senior, as it was called then. But that was just the way it was back then. Only five girls in my class did go on to Senior. Our families weren't wealthy; they needed us to work. I went and learned shorthand and typing and started work as a stenographer as soon as I could.

Win's first job was in the office at a car dealership, where she met her future husband Bruce, who was a salesman. As he headed off to war, she answered an advertisement to join the office staff of the national broadcaster, the ABC.

My job was to organise the rehearsal times for the artists. It was very exciting to be there at that time, during the war. I once had to meet the movie star Gary Cooper and take him up to the studios. Another time General MacArthur came in. I was there for six years.

In 1944 Bruce returned from war and he and Win were married. A year later, pregnant with their daughter Alexis, Win left the ABC and became a full-time mother. Over the next nineteen years Alexis was joined by six brothers and sisters, leaving Win little time to dream of what might have been – yet her ambition of teaching music never left her.

It was something I had always wanted to do. I don't know how my parents afforded it, but they had paid for me to have piano lessons at primary school when I was eight, nine and ten years old. I must have been quite good because when visitors came to the school the teachers always brought me out to play.

When youngest daughter Lisa was five years old Win began to think more seriously about the dream career she had been forced to

abandon. After discussing it with Bruce and the children and getting
a positive response, she decided to pick up where she had left off some
thirty-five years earlier.

'I studied for my Senior Certificate by correspondence through the
Department of Education,' Win said. 'It was a three-year course to cover
the final two years of school.'

Studying was one thing, but sitting for her senior exams, aged 51, in
a school assembly hall filled with seventeen-year-olds was quite another.
To her great joy she was successful in her exams and was accepted into
Teachers College.

It was terribly embarrassing at first. At 52 I was obviously the
oldest one there. The rest were eighteen, nineteen or twenty
years old. Back in those days (1974) mature-age students
weren't as accepted as they are now, so people were quite
taken aback. But after they got used to me they were all very
nice. It was a four-year full-time course and I studied and sat
for my music exam at the same time.

The day I graduated I felt like I had won the lottery. Bruce
and all the children were there. It was a wonderful moment
for me.

It didn't take Win long to come back to earth. She was posted to
a high school and found that schools – and schoolchildren – had changed
a great deal in the forty years since she had been a student.

I was shocked by the lack of respect the children had for
teachers. It was all very different to what I had expected.
I thought the kids would do what they were told to do
straightaway. Some were really quite insolent. I used to tread
on their toes and pretend it was an accident. I'd say 'Oh, I am
sorry'. They soon got the message.

277

One message that Win didn't want the children to get wind of was that, despite her age, she was a novice.

The kids never knew it was my first teaching job. I pretended I'd been doing it all my life – although, in a way, I had been. I had experience that other teachers just starting off didn't have: I'd raised seven children of my own. Even so, the first day I went to work I felt like I was back having my first day at school. It was really quite frightening and it took a while to get used to. The other teachers, once they got used to me and what I was doing, were mostly very nice.

Some of the children, too, became very close.

I was teaching children who had taken music as an elective subject, so they were keen to learn and very good to teach. Some of the others, the ones who had to take music as a general subject . . . well, they were another story.

For Win, though, teaching music proved to be everything she had hoped and when after eight years the time came to leave, she was sad to go.

It was a wonderful time in my life. The other teachers were very nice and the children and I had a lot of fun. We would put on musicals; I loved it. Unfortunately, the regulations said teachers had to retire at 65, so in 1986 I had to go. I wished I didn't have to. I'd still be doing it today if they'd let me.

In a way she is. Win still gives private lessons on a piano in the bedroom of her one-room waterfront apartment. She has 33 students, a drop from her peak of 90.

I feel terribly satisfied. I had the best of both worlds. I was
a mother to seven and then when they started leaving home
I was able to follow my first dream. I had always loved study,
loved working towards a goal. I always felt I would go to
teachers college at some stage, but then the children came
along. With seven children you have to work hard every day –
and you don't always get morning tea like in some jobs.
I wanted to be home with them, but at the same time in the
back of my mind I never forgot about teaching.

I've never regretted anything I've done. I was a bit tentative
when I first started teaching, wondered how I would be able
to cope, but it turned out well. It was very enlightening, and
when Bruce died in 1990 having my music pupils filled some
empty moments.

It has kept me in touch with young people too. Some of
the children I had back in my first years as a high-school
teacher still send me cards and let me know what they are
doing. Some of them have even become teachers themselves.

No, it's been wonderful. I've loved my life. I wouldn't
change a thing.

# further reading

Knowledge is power and certainly this is true in relation to career change. Think of this book as just one part of the process towards achieving your dream. There are many other books and resources available to help you move along the path. The following will help you expand your knowledge and give further insight into specific areas of employment.

## BOOKS

(All are available through Monster.com. Go to http://content. monster.com/bookstore/.)

Anderson, Sandy, *Women in Career and Life Transitions* (Jist Works, 1999).

Berglas, Dr Steven, *Reclaiming the Fire: How successful people overcome burnout* (Random House, 2001).

Helfand, David P., *Career Change: Everything you need to know to meet new challenges and take control of your career* (Vgm Career Horizons, 1999).

Johnson, Spencer & Blanchard, Kenneth H., *Who Moved My Cheese?* (Putnam Publishing Group, 1998).

Kanchier, Carole, *Dare to Change Your Job and Your Life* (Jist Works, 1999).

Krannich, Ronald L., *Change Your Job, Change Your Life: High impact strategies for finding great jobs in the decade ahead* (Impact Publications, 1999).

Lore, Nicholas, *The Pathfinder: How to choose or change your career for a lifetime of satisfaction and success* (Fireside, 1998).

Reinhold, Barbara, *Free to Succeed: Designing the life you want in the new free agent economy,* (Plume, 2001).

Tansey, Elizabeth, *Good News! You're Fired! A comprehensive guide for people in career transition* (Nebbadoon Press, 1998).

## ONLINE RESOURCES

au.eresourcing.tmp.com

www.anzwers.com.au/jobs/

www.careerone.com.au

www.careersonline.com.au

www.civvystreet.com.au (*military to civilian transition*)

www.ecareer.com.au

www.findmycv.com

www.futurestep.com.au

www.getajob.com.au

www.itskillshub.com.au

www.jobfind.com

www.jobsculptor.com

www.JobsDB.com.au

www.jobsearch.gov.au

www.Monster.com

www.mycareer.com.au

www.positionsvacant.com.au

www.recruitersonline.com (*IT industry*)

www.resume.net.au

www.resumenetwork.com.au

www.seek.com.au

www.sportemploymentaustralia.com.au (*sport industry*)

www.sportspeople.com.au (*sport industry*)

www.theshortlist.com.au

www.tourismjobsnetwork.com.au

www.yourportfolio.com.au

**For advice regarding designing electronic resumés**

www.eresumes.com

**To develop interviewing skills**

www.interview.Monster.com

**For information about retraining and higher education**

www.studylink.com.au

# index